Introduction to Environmental Economics and Policy in Japan

Toshi H. Arimura · Akira Hibiki

Introduction to Environmental Economics and Policy in Japan

Springer

Toshi H. Arimura
Faculty of Political Science and Economics
Waseda University
Tokyo, Japan

Akira Hibiki
Graduate School of Economics
and Management
Tohoku University
Sendai, Japan

ISBN 978-981-97-2186-3 ISBN 978-981-97-2187-0 (eBook)
https://doi.org/10.1007/978-981-97-2187-0

Translation from the Japanese language edition: "Nyūmon kankyō keizaigaku, shinpan: Datsu tanso jidai no kadai to saitekikai" by Toshi H. Arimura and Akira Hibiki, © Toshihide Arimura, Akira Hibiki 2023. Published by CHUOKORON-SHINSHA. INC. All Rights Reserved.

This Springer imprint is published by the registered company Springer Nature Singapore Pte Ltd.
The registered company address is: 152 Beach Road, #21-01/04 Gateway East, Singapore 189721, Singapore

Paper in this product is recyclable.

Preface

Environmental problems abound in the world. Air pollution is a big issue in developing economies both outdoors in urban areas and indoors in rural villages. Although making progress on the environment, developed economies are now grappling with issues such as waste management and plastic pollution. International efforts have been made to address climate change since the adoption of the Kyoto Protocol, the world's first agreement to mitigate GHG emissions. Meanwhile, in 2023, we experienced the highest temperature ever recorded since the preindustrial period. We are facing environmental crises. We need solutions to tackle them.

Environmental economics prescribes solutions to environmental issues from the perspective of economics. This book serves as an introduction to environmental economics and provides a lens through which to understand environmental problems and evaluate policy instruments. Many textbooks on environmental economics focus on the context and perspectives of North America and Europe, making the examples less useful for readers in Asia and other developing economies. This book presents a unique approach to environmental economics by drawing on the Japanese experience of environmental problems and policies.

The book is intended to serve as a textbook for introductory courses on environmental economics for undergraduate students. It also serves as a valuable resource for government officials and corporate environmental officers interested in environmental economics. To ensure accessibility to a wide range of readers, the authors intentionally avoid the use of calculus or cumbersome algebra. The book also serves as an introductory reader or textbook on environmental policy in Japan. It explains how the country has been coping with environmental problems that emerging and developing economies currently confront, such as air pollution and improper waste management. We believe that the book is particularly useful for students in Asia and emerging economies that now experience severe environmental problems.

The book is divided into two parts. Part I, which covers Chaps. 1–6, focuses on the theory of environmental economics. Chapter 1 provides an overview of negative externality and Pigouvian tax as a means to achieve the social optimum. Chapter 2 compares market-based policy instruments with command and control regulations.

Chapter 3 examines a property rights approach to environmental issues and the mechanisms of emissions trading schemes. Chapter 4 considers carbon tax and emissions trading schemes as policy choices in the presence of uncertainty. Chapter 5 discusses solid waste management policy with a focus on situations where there are limitations in landfill sites. Chapter 6 explains how liability rules for damages give firms incentives to adopt precautionary measures. We consider the socially optimal level of measures against environmental accidents and institutional designs desirable to achieve that level of measures.

Part II of the book discusses environmental issues and policies in Japan. Chapter 7 introduces Japan's recycling policy and practices. It then focuses on microplastic pollution, a growing environmental concern worldwide, and policy measures recently implemented in Japan to address it. Policy interventions to discourage improper waste disposal and illegal dumping are also discussed in the chapter. Chapter 8 explores air pollution in Japan and around the world. The chapter discusses Japan's policy measures such as sulfur charges and vehicle-type regulations from an economic perspective. Air pollution issues worldwide are then discussed, including household air pollution in developing economies. Chapter 9 provides an overview of international initiatives on climate change, including the Clean Development Mechanism (CDM) and how it led to the emergence of the Joint Crediting Mechanisms (JCM). The chapter discusses the role of carbon pricing in reducing carbon emissions and reviews carbon pricing schemes currently adopted at the regional and national levels in Japan. The prospects of carbon pricing in Japan for carbon neutrality are also discussed.

This book is based on the Japanese book, *Introduction to Environmental Economics*, published by Chuokoron-Shinsha, Inc. While the original book was written for Japanese readers, we have rewritten the entire text to cater to an international audience. Specifically, we made revisions to make the content more relevant to readers in emerging economies in Asia. Additionally, two new chapters have been added to enhance the theoretical framework. One chapter covers liability rules against environmental accidents, while the other focuses on policy instrument choice under uncertainty. Finally, we have updated the examples, data, and policies discussed in Chaps. 7–9.

Numerous revisions and updates were required to compose this book. We would like to express our gratitude to Hanae Katayama and Hajime Katayama for their helpful and insightful comments on all chapters. We owe a lot to Hotaka Kobori for the initial translation. Without him, we would not have been able to produce this book. We would like to thank Aline Mortha and Atsushi Morimoto for their helpful and insightful suggestions, and Guanyu Lu for helping to refine several chapters. Finally, we would like to acknowledge Yayue Xiao for her contribution to finalizing our manuscript.

The completion of this book is based on the past research experiences of the two authors. We have received support from many senior colleagues, including Prof. Kikuo Iwata, to whom Hibiki is indebted, and Prof. Susumu Imai, to whom Arimura is indebted. The authors express their gratitude to them.

This book received support from several research funds and institutes. Akira Hibiki acknowledges the financial support received from JSPS 24K00245, 21H00672, and 18H00839, as well as the Environment Research and Technology Development Fund JPMEERF20S11850 and the Future Creation Fund of the Graduate School of Economics and Management at Tohoku University. Toshi Arimura acknowledges the financial support received from JSPS KAKENHI grant number 21H04945, Waseda Institute for Political Science and Economics, the Foundation of Japanese Bankers, and the English Academic Book Publication Support Subsidy from Waseda University. He also acknowledges the support of the Paris School of Economics and Maison Suger during his sabbatical visit to Paris.

Finally, we would like to dedicate this book to our families. Toshi Arimura finished the manuscript while he was visiting Paris School of Economics during his sabbatical from Waseda University. He appreciates the support from his wife, Michiko Arimura, during this stay. Akira Hibiki also is grateful to his wife, Michiko Hibiki, for her support.

Paris, France — Toshi H. Arimura
Sendai, Japan — Akira Hibiki

Contents

About the Authors

Dr. Toshi H. Arimura is a professor of Political Science and Economics and Director of the Research Institute for Environment Economics and Management at Waseda University in Tokyo. Prior to joining Waseda, he was a professor at Sophia University in Tokyo and was a visiting scholar with George Mason University and Resources for the Future as a recipient of the Abe Fellowship. His research interests include climate change, energy policies, air pollution regulations, and voluntary environmental actions. Dr. Arimura holds a Ph.D. in economics from the University of Minnesota, an M.Sc. in environmental sciences from the University of Tsukuba, and a B.A. in history of science from the University of Tokyo. He has served on a number of Japanese government committees on environmental issues including the committees on carbon pricing (2018) of the environmental council under Ministry of the Environment and on GX-ETS (2022) under Ministry of Economy Trade and Industry. He is currently a visiting scholar at Paris School of Economics and Sciences Po.

Dr. Akira Hibiki is a professor at Graduate School of Economics and Management and a director at Research Center for Policy Design at Tohoku University. He also serves as a head of a Research Group at National Institute for Environmental Studies and a consulting fellow at Research Institute of Economy, Trade, and Industry (RIETI). Prior to joining Tohoku University, he was a professor at Sophia University, a head of Environmental Economics Section at National Institute for Environmental Studies, and an associate professor at the Tokyo Institute of Technology in Japan. He also served as a president of Society for Environmental Economics and Policy Studies in Japan (2018–2020). His research centers on topics related to environmental and resource economics.

Part I
Theory of Environmental Economics

Chapter 1
Environmental Problems: A Market Failure

Toshi H. Arimura

Abstract This chapter presents an economic perspective on environmental problems. Pollution, climate change, and all other environmental problems are considered by economists as negative externalities and market failures. To solve environmental problems, economic activity, which is intrinsically linked with nature and natural resources, needs to be controlled in such a way to achieve a social optimum where social welfare is maximized. A Pigouvian tax that puts prices on negative externalities in the form of environmental taxation is examined in this chapter as an example of environmental policy instruments designed to achieve a social optimum.

Keywords Social surplus · Negative externality · Optimal pollution · Pigouvian tax · Environmental tax · Social cost

1.1 Consumer Benefit and Producer Benefit: Understanding Demand Curve and Supply Curve

Imagine you are sitting in a coffee shop with a cup of coffee in hand, flipping through the pages of this book. This one cup of coffee contains the basic elements of environmental economics. You (the consumer) derive a certain level of satisfaction from the consumption of a cup of coffee. The coffee shop (the producer) is also making some profit by selling a cup of coffee. The burning of gas to boil water for the coffee leads to the emission of carbon dioxide, which causes climate change. A cup of coffee has a lot to do with the benefits of consumers and producers and even environmental issues.

Just like this coffee analogy, the economic activities of consumers and producers, and environmental issues associated with coffee consumption can be viewed on the same footing; this is what environmental economics does. Economics, contrary to what the word sounds like, is not about making money. It studies the roles of the market and government in achieving a desirable society. Using the framework of economics, both environmental issues and economic activities can be understood within a unified framework.

T. H. Arimura and A. Hibiki, *Introduction to Environmental Economics and Policy in Japan*, https://doi.org/10.1007/978-981-97-2187-0_1

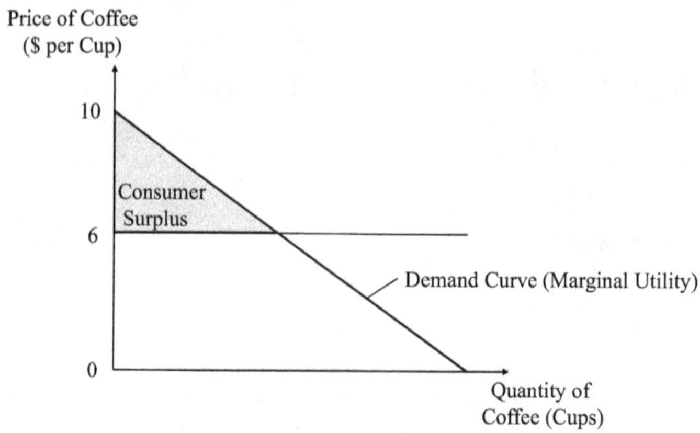

Fig. 1.1 Demand curve and consumer surplus for a cup of coffee. (*Note* The value on the *y*-axis [the price of coffee] determines the value on the *x*-axis [the quantity demanded])

What approach does economics use to clarify the roles of the market and government? This chapter will start with a review of fundamental concepts in economics (e.g., consumer behavior, producer behavior, supply and demand in the market), as they are essential for examining environmental problems from an economic perspective. We will then discuss how markets alone cannot solve environmental problems and consider effective policy options. Readers who already have a basic knowledge of microeconomics may skip this chapter and go on to Chap. 2.

1.1.1 Consumption of Goods and Consumer Benefits: Consumer Surplus

Even if you have never studied economics, you may have seen a diagram of the supply curve and the demand curve, where the price is determined at the intersection of two lines, as shown in Fig. 1.1. Let us first consider the demand curve to understand the consumer's behavior. In economics, products and services that individuals consume are called **goods**. The curve that expresses the relationship between the price and the quantity demanded for the good is called the **demand curve**. As shown in the figure, it is represented by a curve that falls to the right.[1] This curve shows that, as prices fall, the quantity demanded increases.

Why do people consume goods in the first place? An economist's answer would be that it is because people receive **utility** (**benefits**) from their consumption. Suppose a coffee lover is willing to pay up to three dollars for a cup of coffee. This means the benefits from a cup of coffee are worth three dollars to this person. The utility

[1] In this book, both the demand and supply curves are represented by straight lines. However, in general, they are not necessarily straight lines.

obtained from one incremental unit of the good, a cup of coffee in this case, is called the **marginal utility** (also known as **marginal benefits**). Marginal utility generally decreases as the consumption of the good increases (which is called **diminishing marginal utility**).

Suppose you walk into a coffee shop and have a cup of coffee for three dollars. It was delicious, and you want to have more. But also suppose that you do not feel like paying three dollars for the second cup, so you leave the coffee shop. Economics explains this behavior as follows: the first coffee was purchased because its marginal utility is higher or the same as the actual price. However, you did not buy the second cup because the marginal utility was lower than the actual price. In other words, buying only one cup is a sign of diminishing marginal utility at individual level. If we aggregate individual demand curves, we can derive the downward sloping demand curve at the market level.

One could also explain the downward sloping demand curve at the market level as follows. For simplicity, suppose that each individual can have just one cup of coffee. The marginal utility of coffee varies across individuals. It may be zero for those who do not like coffee but remarkably high for those who love coffee. The varying marginal utilities are arranged from left to right in descending order of magnitude, and naturally, the demand curve is a downward sloping (in other words, the demand curve = marginal utility).

Sometimes you get more utility (benefit) than you paid for. Suppose that you desperately want coffee. There is an expensive-looking coffee shop in front of you, where a cup of coffee costs about ten dollars. But, because you really need a cup of coffee, you decide to go into the shop. Comfortable sofas and spacious tables with classical music playing in the background. You open the menu and are surprised to find that the coffee is only six dollars! You enjoy the cup of coffee with great satisfaction.

Here, we are seeing the following economic phenomenon. You really wanted coffee and your marginal utility of a coffee was ten dollars, but since the actual price was six dollars, you derive additional satisfaction from paying a price lower than expected. We can think of this four-dollar difference ($10 – $6) as a gain. This difference is called **surplus** (surplus = marginal utility – price). The sum of these gains for each individual in society is called **consumer surplus**. We can express consumer surplus as the difference between the demand curve and the price paid for a product. The consumer surplus of society as a whole corresponds to the gray triangular area in Fig. 1.1. In general, the lower the price, the higher the consumer surplus.

The shape of the demand curve is determined by a variety of factors. For example, consider gasoline, which is inseparable from environmental problems. If an alternative fuel for gasoline becomes cheaper, the demand for that fuel will increase and the demand for gasoline will decrease. In other words, the demand curve for gasoline moves downward. Conversely, the demand curve shifts upward if, for example, people's incomes increase and more people own cars, resulting in an increased demand for gasoline. A demand curve is formulated by taking out just two dimensions—the price and quantity demanded—while taking various factors into account.

1.1.2 Production of Goods and Producer Profit: Producer Surplus

Now, we turn to the behavior of producers. We will continue with gasoline as an example. For consumers to consume gasoline, there must be producers to produce it. To understand the behavior of producers, we use the **supply curve**. The supply curve represents the relationship between the price and the goods sold to the market. If the price rises, firms will increase their production in anticipation of profits. If the price falls, they will reduce production by, for example, shortening factory hours. As a result, the supply curve slopes upward to the right, as illustrated in Fig. 1.2.

Suppose that a gas station that opens during the day on weekdays wants to increase its sales. The owner may open the business until late at night or on weekends. However, hiring people to work late at night or on weekends would require paying higher than normal wages. If gasoline sales per unit of time on weekends are the same or lower than on weekdays, the additional cost required to obtain a certain amount of sales will be higher than before.

The incremental cost required to increase the production (in this case, sales) of a good by one additional unit is called the **marginal cost**. As illustrated in the example of the gas station, the marginal cost increases as a firm's production increases. If the marginal cost is less than the price, then the firm can increase its profits by increasing its production volume. This means that a firm can maximize profits by producing at the output level where the marginal cost equals the price. It should be also noted that the marginal cost curve also tells us at what level of output the firm can maximize profits for a given price. Hence, the marginal cost curve of the firm represents the supply curve of the firm. The idea can be applied to the market as a whole; the **marginal cost curve of the market** is the **supply curve of the market**.

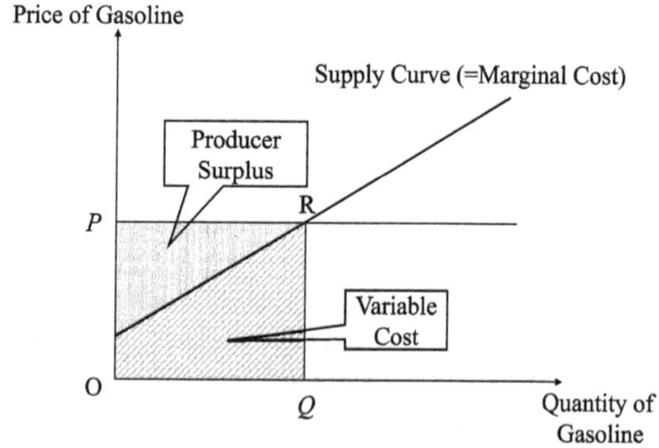

Fig. 1.2 Supply curve and producer surplus

Using the supply curve, we can explain a firm's profit (or gain) from production and its behavior. Since the supply curve is a marginal cost curve, the area underneath the supply curve in Fig. 1.2 represents the **variable cost** of production. When the price is P, the quantity supplied is Q, and the shaded area represents the cost. Since the value of sales in the market is P × Q, it corresponds to just the rectangular area (area OPRQ). Therefore, the gray area, which is sales minus the variable cost of production, corresponds to the producer's "gain." This gain is equivalent to the firm's profit before subtracting **fixed costs** (e.g., plant and equipment, rent for the store), and it is called **producer surplus**. Producer surplus generally increases with higher prices.

1.2 Why Are Markets Omnipotent?

1.2.1 Output and Price Decisions

Next, we use the supply and demand curves to show how the output and the price are determined in the market. In this book, we consider a **competitive market**, in which firms participating in a market act competitively, meaning that one firm cannot determine the price of a product solely on its own initiative. Even if a firm tries to sell for two dollars what others are selling for a dollar, consumers will still be able to buy the good for a dollar. In other words, no firm can ignore the prices of others.

We can find the equilibrium price and output in the market by drawing the supply and demand curves on a single graph, as depicted in Fig. 1.3. The **equilibrium price** is a price that balances the quantity supplied and the quantity demanded. Let P_1 be the market price. Then the demand curve determines the quantity demanded in the market at Q_1, while the supply curve determines the quantity supplied in the market at Q_3. The quantity supplied (Q_3) being greater than the quantity demanded (Q_1) causes a huge excess supply. The price of the good will then fall to sell the inventory at a lower price.

To what extent does the price need to fall to balance demand and supply in the market? If the price is P_2, then, contrary to what we saw earlier, the quantity supplied (Q_2) is less than the quantity demanded (Q_3). In this case, a shortage of the goods occurs, and consumers will be willing to pay a little more for them, so prices will rise. Demand and supply coincide and balance at Q_0, the point where the demand and supply curves intersect, i.e., when the price is P_0. A state of balance between supply and demand is called the **market equilibrium,** and the price at the market equilibrium is called the equilibrium price.

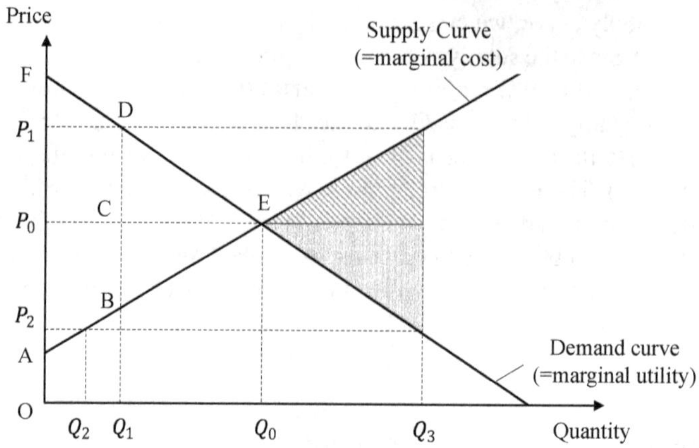

Fig. 1.3 Market equilibrium and social surplus

1.2.2 Socially Optimal Output

Moving away from market mechanism, we now consider the level of output that is optimal (or desirable) from society's point of view. In general, economists consider that society consists of consumers and producers. Hence, economists pursue policies and institutions that can maximizes the benefit for society, which is the sum of the consumers' benefit and producers' benefit.

If we increase the production of goods and provide them to consumers, the consumer's utility will increase. However, the production of goods requires costs. From a social point of view, it is necessary to consider not only the consumer's utility but also the cost and benefits of producers. The **social surplus** involved in the consumption and production of a good is the sum of the consumer surplus (benefits to consumers) and the producer surplus (benefits to the producer).

Let us consider the output level that maximizes social surplus (i.e., consumer surplus + producer surplus) by using Fig. 1.3. Let Q_1 denote the total output in the market. If the price is P_0, then the consumer surplus is represented by area P_0CDF, and the producer surplus by area P_0ABC. Is this output level (Q_1) socially optimal? No, because both the producer and consumer surpluses could increase further by slightly increasing production, which can be done without making any consumers and firms worse off. In other words, point Q_1 is inefficient because it does not realize a socially feasible surplus.

Then, what is the optimal level of output that maximizes social surplus? Suppose that the current output is Q_0. If the output level becomes slightly larger, the marginal cost at that output level will exceed the marginal utility. For example, if production and consumption were to increase to Q_3, the marginal utility would be less than P_0 (This is equivalent to the demand curve falling to the right). If the price remains at

P_0, then the consumer is willing to pay is P_2, which is less than the price P_0. So, the consumer surplus will be reduced by the solid gray area.

On the producer's side, the cost (P_1) exceeds the price (P_0) as production increases to Q_3. As a result, the producer surplus also decreases by the amount of the striped gray area. Thus, when production exceeds Q_0, both consumer and producer surpluses decrease, and so does society's overall surplus. Here, the marginal cost is greater than the marginal utility, which means that you invest more than $10,000 to earn $10,000. Obviously, increasing production above Q_0 is not socially desirable. It is at Q_0 where the social surplus is maximized.

Let us recall the market equilibrium from our earlier discussion. In a competitive market, when price is P_0, output and consumption are in equilibrium at Q_0. Now, we can see Q_0 is exactly the socially optimal output.

It should be noted that at this level of output, the marginal cost of all firms is equal to the price because the condition for a firm to maximize its profit is to produce at the point where its marginal cost and the price are equal. Recall also that the marginal utility of every individual coincides with the price. Hence, social surplus is maximized when the price, marginal cost, and marginal utility are equal (price = marginal cost = marginal utility).

In a competitive market, the socially desirable output is naturally achieved by consumers buying as many goods as they want and by firms pursuing profit. The market is efficient in the sense that social surplus is maximized without government interventions and regulations.

1.3 Why Do Environmental Problems Persist? a Market Failure

So far, we understand that the market economy maximizes social surplus. Can we then leave everything to the market? Should the government play any role in the behavior of businesses and consumers?

Market prices and output do not necessarily reflect all the factors associated with production and consumption. Production and consumption activities of a firm or individual may affect another firm or individual outside the market transaction. In that case, there is an **externality** in the sense that firms and consumers have an effect on others outside (or external to) the market. Although our discussion so far has ignored this problem, environmental and pollution problems are exactly this externality problem. Let us consider the social surplus in the presence of externalities.

1.3.1 External Costs

When gasoline is burned, carbon dioxide is emitted as a byproduct. Consumers of gasoline pay a price for gasoline but not for the byproduct. Climate change caused by carbon dioxide will lead to a rapid climate change and a variety of damages to the environment, which are not traded in the market but directly affect the victims of the environmental damages. These costs (in this case, climate change damage, health costs due to air pollution) that occur external to the market are referred to as **external costs** (or **external diseconomies or negative externalities**).

In a competitive market economy, even when people act in their own self-interest and companies pursue only their own profits, the socially desirable output is still achieved. However, this holds only in the absence of externalities like environmental problems. In a competitive market, what is external to the market (e.g., the consumption of gasoline causing climate change through byproduct carbon dioxide) is not considered. Producers are not likely to refrain from selling gasoline by considering the damage caused by climate change while having no quid pro quo. Likewise, few consumers would cut back on their gasoline purchases because they are concerned about the damage. That's because the damage is incurred outside the market transaction and not reflected onto prices. Some firms and consumers who are particularly concerned about the environment may take individual initiatives to reduce their gasoline consumption. However, unless the initiative is integrated in society at large, its effectiveness will be limited. As environmental problems are external to the market, they cannot be solved by market forces alone. In this sense, environmental problems are an example of a "**market failure**,[2]" a flaw in the market mechanism.

Box 1.1 Public Goods

Environmental problems persist in the marketplace owing to the characterization of environmental goods as public goods. For instance, people from urban areas with heavy traffic pollution travel to national parks with healthy environments for clean air. This is an example of goods (clean air) consumption.

How does clean air consumption differ from gasoline consumption? One person's clean air consumption does not reduce another's consumption. Therefore, people can enjoy the same clean air simultaneously. However, the same gasoline cannot be consumed by two people. This is called consumption rivalry. Clean air does not have rivalry characteristics; it is **non-rivalrous** in consumption.

Additionally, gasoline consumption can be prohibited to an individual, which is called the excludability of consumption. Meanwhile, clean air consumption cannot be prevented. Therefore, clean air possesses the **non-excludability** characteristic.

---

[2] Another example of market failure is public goods. Please read Box 1.1 in this chapter for the definition on public goods.

Goods satisfying the conditions of non-rivalry and non-excludability are called **public goods**. Clean air is a public good that benefits people. However, there are also **negative public goods** which costs people. Climate change is a negative public good satisfying these two characteristics. The rising water levels in Bangladesh does not reduce those of that in Netherlands (non-rivalry). In addition, no country is immune from the damage caused by climate change (non-excludability).

Conversely, climate change mitigation is a positive public good that mitigates climate change damage, a negative public good. Ratifying the Kyoto Protocol and reducing greenhouse gas emissions will mitigate climate change and benefit all countries (non-rivalry). Additionally, it is impossible to exclude certain countries from benefiting (non-excludability).

This is where the issue of **free riding** might occur, in which some countries benefit from other countries' initiative to reduce greenhouse gas emissions but refuse to participate in climate change mitigation. If climate change mitigation is not equally implanted and reliance on others increase, it may discourage climate change mitigation among countries.

The United States (US) withdrew from the Kyoto Protocol, claiming that developing countries are free riders as only industrialized countries are obligated to combat climate change. Therefore, US also free-rides on the precautionary efforts of other developed countries. If all countries followed US, we would not benefit from the positive public good of climate change mitigation and suffer from climate change. Thus, positive public goods should not be supplied in a competitive market where people pursue their own interests. As environmental problems are considered public goods problems, the market is likely to suffer excessive environmental damage.

1.4 Economic Analysis of Environmental Problems

1.4.1 Social Loss in a Competitive Market

We have written that environmental issues are external to the market transaction and can cause harm to third parties who are not consumers or producers, but should we eliminate all external costs of pollution and environmental contamination? Should we aim for so-called "zero emissions" immediately, completely eliminating emissions altogether? We will answer these questions using the concept of social surplus.

Figure 1.4 illustrates gasoline consumption and the external cost of climate change resulting from the consumption. Gasoline consumption is expressed in the horizontal axis and the **marginal external cost** of the climate change damage (i.e., external cost that incurs as gasoline consumption increases by one unit) is expressed in the

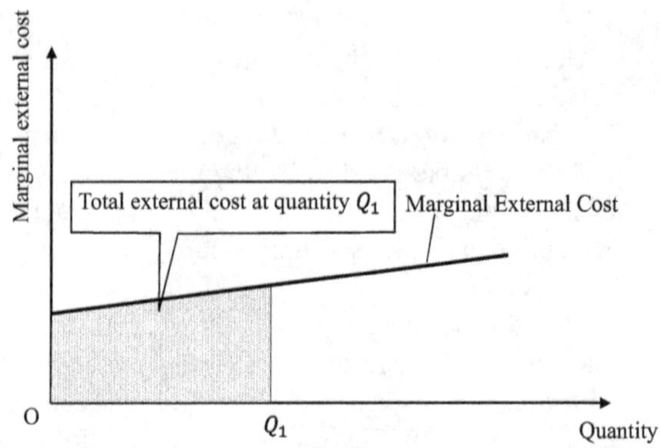

Fig. 1.4 Marginal external cost

vertical axis. Similar to the relationship between total and marginal costs of a firm as described above, the area under the marginal external cost curve corresponds to the total external cost. The more production increases, the more the total external costs grow.

By drawing the marginal external cost curve in Fig. 1.3, we can see the inefficiency of a competitive market in the presence of externalities, as illustrated in Fig. 1.5.

The costs of production on the part of the firm are called **private costs** to distinguish them from external costs. From a social perspective, the costs of producing a good include not only the private costs paid by the producer but also include external costs incurred by environmental problems. The sum of these private costs and external costs is called **social costs**. In a similar vein, the sum of marginal costs and marginal external costs is called **marginal social costs**, as illustrated in Fig. 1.5. When output is at Q_0, the social surplus is the sum of the producer and consumer surpluses (area KBC) if there are no external costs. However, given the climate change problem, we must subtract the external costs from the sum of the production and consumer surplus to compute the total surplus. Hence, the social surplus is the sum of the producer and consumer surpluses minus the external costs (i.e., area KBC—area KBDF) when output is Q_0. Here, a portion of the producer surplus and consumer

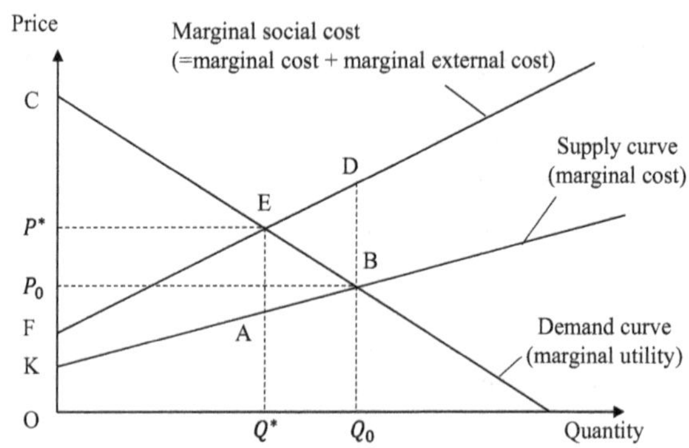

Fig. 1.5 A market with externalities

surplus will offset the external costs of the environmental problem for the amount indicated by area KBEF. As a result, the social surplus is area FEC—area EBD. We can see that the social surplus is reduced by the presence of externalities.

1.4.2 Optimal Levels of Output and Pollution: Social Surplus Maximization

What is the optimal level of output when external costs like environmental problems are present? If we rely on the market mechanism, the external costs (i.e., environmental problems) will be excessive. Let us consider point E in Fig. 1.5 to find the answer. If the output supplied in the market is Q*, then the price is P*. The size of the consumer surplus is area P*EC, and the producer surplus is area KAEP*. In other words, the size of the consumer and producer surpluses combined is area KAEC. In this case, the magnitude of the external cost is area KAEF, so the social surplus is area KAEC—area KAEF = area FEC. Now, recall that the social surplus in the market equilibrium was area FEC—area EBD. By reducing output from Q_0 (the market equilibrium) to Q*, the social surplus increases by area EBD. It turns out that the social surplus is maximized at point Q* where the marginal utility (i.e., the height of the demand curve) equals the marginal cost plus the marginal external cost, namely, the marginal social cost.

Notice that the climate change problem has not been solved entirely, as the damage caused by climate change still exists (area KAEF). However, any further reduction in output will cause greater reduction in the benefits to consumers and producers than the reduction in damage. As a result, society will be negatively affected overall.

Social surplus is maximized when output is determined at Q*, while, in a competitive market, the consumption and production of goods that causes environmental problems will be excessive. Without government interventions, extra output will be produced as indicated by the difference between Q_0 and Q*. As a result, even though corporate profits increase, social surplus is lost by the amount of area EBD. This loss precisely corresponds to the loss to society due to environmental problems.

1.4.3 Is Achieving Zero Emissions the Right Thing to Do?

The term “zero emissions” has often been used as a keyword for solving environmental problems. The idea is to reduce waste and pollution to zero. In our gasoline example, zero emissions would mean zero gasoline use. In that case, the climate change damage caused by gasoline use may be reduced to zero. However, if this happens immediately, the profits of firms (producer surplus) from producing gasoline will also go to zero and so will the benefit of consumers (consumer surplus) from using gasoline. Many consumers would not agree with zero gasoline consumption (i.e., no benefit from the consumption) while recognizing the importance of environmental initiatives. For the sake of the argument, we assume in this chapter that there would be no change in technology. Technological advancements might enable us to achieve near zero emissions without reducing gasoline consumption. However, it is important to consider how much it will cost to develop the technology because zero emissions at an overly high cost would not be socially desirable, at least, in the short run.

1.5 How Can a Market Failure Be Solved?

1.5.1 Regulatory Instruments and Market-Based Instruments (Economic Instruments)

So far, we understood that the production of goods with external costs can be excessive and cause environmental problems if we rely on the market mechanism. It is desirable to reduce output to Q* (Fig. 1.5) by some means, and government intervention is needed to tackle environmental problems.

Here, the government can take two approaches. One is a **regulatory instrument**. In the simplest form, the government directly controls the output and pollution levels produced by firms. The other is a **market-based instrument (economic instrument)** with which the government aims to reduce pollution by exploiting the profit-seeking attitude of firms. Let us consider each of them below.

1.5.2 Administrative Solutions: Command and Control Regulation

With regulatory measures, the government directly regulates the producers and consumers who are responsible for the environmental problems. It is also known as **command and control** regulation in the example of climate change caused by gasoline consumption, one way is to limit the total amount of gasoline sold. That is, the government controls the output of gasoline in society as a whole as not to exceed Q*. Then, no matter how much price rises, firms cannot increase their production. In this case, the supply curve is perpendicular to horizontal axis at Q*, as illustrated in Fig. 1.6. The equilibrium price is P* where the demand and supply curves intersect as shown in the figure. The price is higher than it was before the regulation was imposed. As a result, the consumer surplus becomes smaller than it was before the implementation (area P*EC). If there is no income transfer, such as compensation for climate change damage, then the producer surplus is area KAEP*, which is not necessarily smaller than before the regulation took place. The damage from

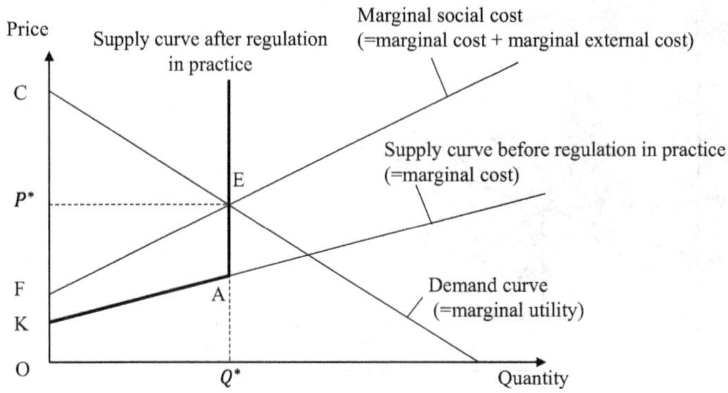

Fig. 1.6 Regulatory instruments

climate change remains as indicated by area KAEF. However, the social surplus is maximized, as indicated by area FEC.

Here, notice that the climate change damage by gasoline consumption is not borne by the firms producing and selling gasoline. It is the victims of the environmental harm who bear the cost. Of course, the government could oblige firms to compensate for the damage. In this case, too, it is sensible to choose Q* that maximizes social surplus.

1.5.3 The Tax Solution

Market-based instruments are designed to achieve a social optimum by exploiting the behaviors of profit-seeking producers and utility-maximizing consumers that cause environmental problems. An example of this approach is an **environmental tax**, which is a fee charged to the polluter that depends on the quantity of pollutants they release. A per unit tax should be set equal to the marginal external cost at the socially desirable output Q*; the per unit tax should be the line EA, as illustrated in Fig. 1.7. Now let t* denote the magnitude of this tax.

The taxed firm will decrease its output because its marginal cost will rise by the amount t*. By recalling that the supply curve = marginal cost, we see the supply curve in the market will move up by t* as a result of taxation. To what extent does the market reduce output overall? The supply curve after taxation intersects the demand curve at P*. That is, the equilibrium price after taxation is P* and the amount of output is reduced to Q* (from Q_0 in Fig. 1.5).

In this case, the consumer surplus is equal to the size of area P*EC, which is the same as that in the case of the regulatory instrument. The difference is that by imposing the tax, the government increases its revenue by the size of area KAEG. As a result of the environmental tax, the producer surplus is area GEP*, which is smaller than in the case of the regulatory instrument. Note, however, that tax revenues will

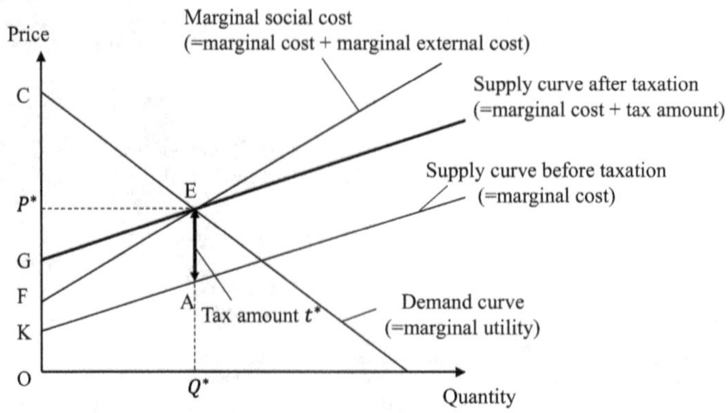

Fig. 1.7 Environmental taxation

be returned to consumers, producers, or the victims of the environmental harm. As a result, the magnitude of the social surplus subtracting external cost from the sum of producer surplus, consumer surplus and tax revenue[3], which is area FEC. Hence, the size of the social surplus would not change with either a tax or a regulatory instrument.

However, the consumer and the producer surpluses will vary depending on how the government distributes the tax revenue. The revenue can also be used to compensate the victims. This distinguishes taxation from regulatory measures where the victims bear the cost of environmental harm.

Environmental taxes put prices on environmental pollution and damages in the form of taxation. They are designed to internalize negative externalities associated with the pollution and damages. Firms are then induced to take account of these externalities in their production decisions. This is called the **internalization of externalities**. Environmental taxes are designed to maximize social surplus by appealing to profit-orientated firms to reduce their impact on the environment.

1.5.4 The Subsidy Solution

Another economic tool is the use of subsidies. It is a policy instrument to give polluters an environmental subsidy if they reduce their production. The subsidy gives firms incentives to do so because by reducing their production, they can decrease their costs and they even get subsidized by doing so. It is optimal to give a subsidy equal to the amount of the tax we just imposed (t*) for each reduction in the release of pollution. Then the output level that is in equilibrium output will be reduced to Q*,

---

[3] We can write as follows; (Social Surplus) = (Producer surplus) + (Consumer Surplus) + (Tax Revenue) – (External Costs).

which is the point where the social surplus is maximized. It may be worth pointing out that subsidies are against the polluter pays principle despite their effectiveness.

1.5.5 Implementation Issues

The regulatory and market-based instruments share one major drawback: they both assume that policymakers can accurately estimate external costs. On the one hand, it is possible to estimate the demand and supply curves based on factors like market prices prior to the introduction of environmental policies. On the other hand, it may be difficult, if not impossible, to accurately quantify the cost of environmental problems,[4] i.e., how much people are inconvenienced by them. Therefore, environmental policies in practice may not always be implemented in a way that maximizes social surplus.

Box 1.2 Economic Evaluation of the Environment

To solve environmental problems, internalization, which is internalizing external environment into the market, as an economic solution is necessary. Additionally, in internalization, a price must be attached to the environment. In environmental economics, the amount of money people are willing to pay to protect a certain environment is called **Willingness to Pay (WTP)**.

Measuring WTP in an environment is a difficult task due to the following reasons: First, market prices for the environment do not exist as it is an external factor. Therefore, prices are indicated outside the market. Second, as the environment is considered a public good, free riding might occur and WTP will be difficult to obtain. Therefore, this raises questions such as what methods can determine the economic value of the environment?

The **revealed preference method** uses people's WTP indirectly expressed in the market. The **hedonic method**, which is a part of this category, estimates WTP for environmental quality from asset prices. For instance, to what extent do people value "quietness"? This may sound like a difficult task but people indirectly reveal their WTP for quietness in the market. For example, quiet residential areas are more popular than noisy areas and people's preferences for quietness are reflected in land prices. Therefore, the hedonic method attempts to estimate WTP for environmental quality. Furthermore, land prices do not solely depend on noise level but also on various factors such as distance to the nearest station and town center. Land prices can be classified into these factors and WTP for quietness can be determined.

[4] Those who are interested in how to estimate the monetary value of the environment, please read Appendix 2 in this chapter. Kolstad (2010) and Managi and Kuriyama (2017) offer theory and methodology more in details.

The **travel cost method**, another commonly used revealed preference method, measures the value of sites, such as national parks, based on the behavior of people visiting them. People travel to national parks, shoulder transportation costs, and pay entrance fees. This shows that the value of national parks surpass its incurred costs. Utilizing this information to estimate people's WTP for a park forms the basis of the travel cost method.

Contrastingly, the **stated preference method** involves the direct expression of people's environmental values. The **contingent valuation method** (CVM) is a typical approach. A hypothetical questionnaire was used to determine people's WTP to preserve their actual environment. Researchers conducted **choice experiments** to reveal respondents' preferences by presenting multiple options with different environmental attributes.

Readers can refer to Kolstad (2010) and Managi and Kuriyama (2017) for further details.

References

Kolstad, C. (2010) Environmental Economics 2nd (second) Edition. Oxford University Press: New York, Oxford.

Managi, S. and Kuriyama, K. (2017) Environmental Economics. Routledge

Chapter 2
Choice of Policy Instruments: Tax, Regulation or Subsidy

Akira Hibiki

Abstract In this chapter, we consider three policy instruments: environmental taxes, regulations, and subsidies. We first show that environmental taxes are preferable to regulations. When the government implements a regulatory instrument and assigns an optimal production volume to each firm in a way to minimize the sum of variable costs of the market, it may misallocate the volume due to limited data available for policymaking and thus, the total variable costs of the market are not likely to be minimized. With environmental taxation, however, the total variable costs are minimized by the market mechanism. We then show that environmental taxes are preferable to subsidies in the long term when firms enter or exit from the industry. Environmental taxation imposes higher tax payments on higher-polluting firms, thereby lowering their profit margins. Consequently, they withdraw from the industry, which results in inducing the industry to lower its environmental impact. This long-term policy effect is less likely to occur by the introduction of a subsidy.

Keywords Social surplus · Environmental tax · Regulation · Subsidy · Cost minimization

In the 1960s, while Japan was enjoying high economic growth, environmental problems became salient. Pollutants emitted from production plants caused pollution diseases such as Itai-itai disease, Yokkaichi asthma, and Minamata disease. At the time, the government adopted regulatory measures and thereby controlled the amount of exhaust gas emitted into the air and the concentration of pollutants in wastewater. Since then, regulatory measures have played a central role in environmental protection in Japan. In the 1980s, when global environmental issues emerged and became a concern worldwide, economic instruments such as environmental taxes and emissions trading schemes started to draw an increasing amount of attention as an alternative to regulatory measures. This is because economic instruments, such as environmental taxes, are less costly means to reduce pollutants than traditional regulatory instruments.

In Chap. 1, we discussed policy instruments that aim to achieve socially optimal output in cases where environmental externalities arise from firms' production. It

T. H. Arimura and A. Hibiki, *Introduction to Environmental Economics and Policy in Japan*, https://doi.org/10.1007/978-981-97-2187-0_2

was discussed that whichever instruments—regulatory instruments, environmental taxes, and subsidy schemes—could maximize social surplus. In practice, however, environmental taxes are considered to be a preferable instrument to subsidy schemes and regulatory instruments. One of the reasons, as will be pointed out in Section II, is the regulatory inefficiencies caused by government failure. We will also explain differences in impact on the industry structure across different policy schemes.

2.1 Environmental Taxes

In a competitive market, each firm chooses the output level that maximizes its own profit and the sum of all firms' production costs (i.e., the production cost in the market as a whole) will be minimized at that output level. Environmental taxes exploit these profit-maximizing behaviors of firms and guide the total output in the market to an optimal level by reducing each firm's production. In this section, we will see how an environmental tax minimizes the cost of production in the market at the output level chosen by each firm.

In Fig. 2.1, where the vertical (horizontal) axis represents the price (the output), an environmental tax is implemented in such a way that the output achieves an optimal level. In the figure, the curve D is the demand curve for the good. The curve S is the supply curve before the tax is imposed, also representing a market marginal cost (MC curve). The curve S′ is the supply curve after the tax (t*) is imposed. MSC represents the marginal social cost curve, i.e., the sum of a marginal cost (MC) and marginal external cost (MEC) for each level of output. As we saw in Chap. 1, the optimal output is Q*, the optimal environmental tax is t* (per unit of the good), and the price of the good including the tax is P*.

Here we address the quantity each firm produces at price P* and the associated cost of production. For simplicity, suppose that there are only two firms, firms A and

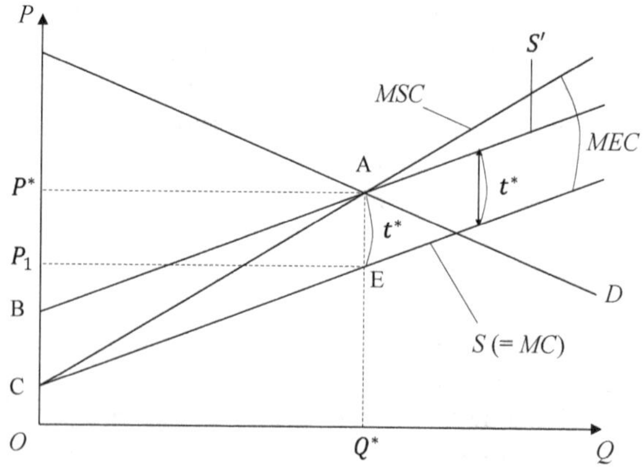

Fig. 2.1 Environmental taxes and optimal output

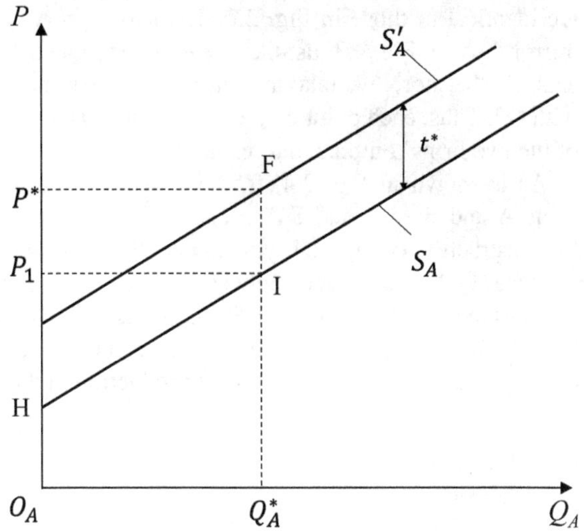

Fig. 2.2 Firm A's supply curve and output

B, in the market. In Fig. 2.2 (2.3), the curves S_A and S_A' (S_B and S_B') represent A's (B's) supply curves before and after the tax is imposed, respectively. As you see in the figures, the tax shifts S_A and S_B up by t* to S_A' and S_B', respectively. The reason for this shift is that for the firms to supply the same quantity as before the tax was levied, the after-price must equal the before-tax price *plus the tax*; otherwise, the after-price minus the tax (i.e., how much the firm receives by selling one unit of the good) will not be equal to the before-tax price.

At the market price (including the tax) of P*, firms A and B produce Q_A* and Q_B*, respectively. For these outputs, $Q_A^* + Q_B^* = Q^*$ must hold (in equilibrium, the sum of the firms' outputs equals the market output); otherwise, Q* would not be an equilibrium output. For each firm's output, then, how much is the associated production cost? As the before-tax supply curve of firm A is its marginal cost curve, the variable cost of firm A is represented by area O_AHI Q_A*. Similarly, the variable cost for firm B corresponds to area O_BLK Q_B*. The sum of the two areas is the total variable cost in the market. It should be noted that the same cost can also be represented by area OCEQ* in Fig. 2.1 by using the market marginal cost curve (MC curve).

We next address whether and how the variable cost[1] depends on the allocation of output produced by the two firms, given the total output of the market being Q*. For this analysis, we will use Fig. 2.4 that combines Figs. 2.2 and 2.3 in a particular manner. In the figure, O_A is taken as the origin for firm A; firm A's output is measured horizontally *left to right*. The supply curves for firm A (i.e., S_A and S_A')

[1] We focus on the variable cost rather than the total production cost in this chapter. When the variable cost is minimized, the production cost is also minimized. This is because the production cost is equal to the variable cost plus the fixed cost which is not changed, when the allocation of output is changed.

are identical to those in Fig. 2.2. The supply curves for firm B (i.e., S_B and S_B') mirror those in Fig. 2.3 just like the figure is rotated 180 degrees around the vertical axis. Furthermore, we take the interval between the origins O_A and O_B to coincide with Q*. Thus, each point on the horizontal axis represents a particular combination of the two firms' outputs that result in the total output of Q*.

As is shown in Fig. 2.4, it is at price P* that the after-tax supply curves for firms A and B (S_A' and S_B', respectively) intersect with each other. This occurs by construction of Fig. 2.4; you can confirm that at the market price of P*, firm A produces Q_A* (the distance between O_A and M) as in Fig. 2.2, firm B produces Q_B* (the distance between O_B and M) as in Fig. 2.3, and the sum of the firms' output, $Q_A* + Q_B*$, is equal to Q* (the distance between O_A and O_B) as in Fig. 2.1. You can also see that the variable cost of production in the market is represented by area

Fig. 2.3 Firm B's supply curve and output

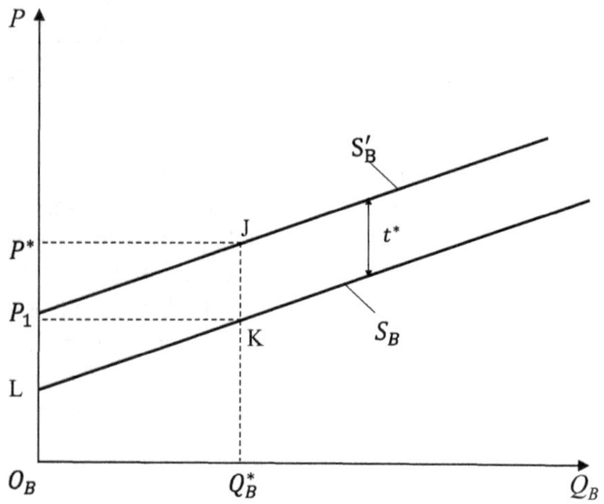

Fig. 2.4 Market prices and allocation of output between firms A and B

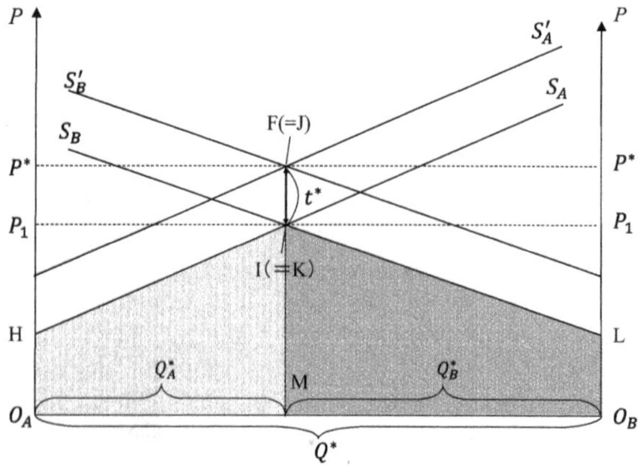

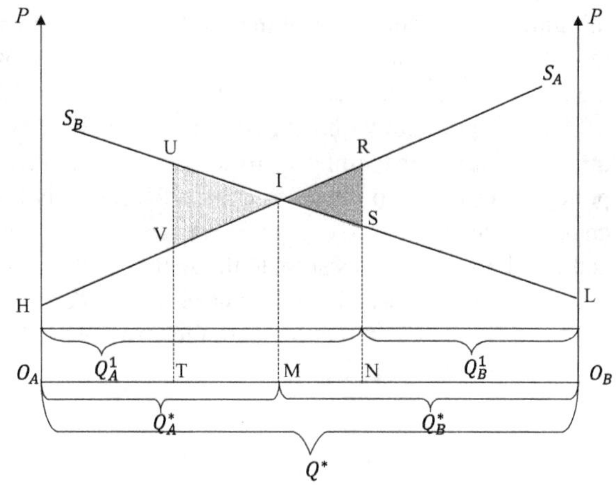

Fig. 2.5 Change in the allocation of output between firm A and B and change in the total variable costs

O_AHILO_B, which is the sum of area O_AHIM (the variable cost for firm A) and area O_BLIM (i.e., the variable cost for firm B).

Using Fig. 2.4, we can show that the variable cost of the production in the market is minimized when firms A and B produce Q_A* and Q_B*, respectively (where the variable cost is represented by area O_AHILO_B). In other words, when the firms' output levels are other than indicated by point M, the variable cost becomes larger even if the total output remains the same. Figure 2.5 is a simplified version of Fig. 2.4, leaving out S_A' and S_B', as they are irrelevant for our discussion. Now, consider point N (that is, a point to the right of point M), the combination of the firms' output levels where firm A produces $Q_A{}^1$ and firm B produces $Q_B{}^1$. Firm A's variable cost is area O_AHRN, firm B's variable cost is area O_BLSN, and therefore, the total cost of production in the market is: area O_AHRN + area O_BLSN = area O_AHILO_B + area IRS. In other words, the variable cost is larger by area IRS when the output levels are those indicated by point N than when indicated by point M.

Why does the variable cost increase? It is because the marginal cost of firm A exceeds the marginal cost of firm B; at point N, the marginal cost of firm A is RN and the marginal cost of firm B is SN. If we compare the increase in variable costs resulting from producing one additional unit of output, it is larger for firm A than for firm B at point N. Therefore, if firm A reduces production and firm B increases production by the amount that firm A reduces, the variable cost in the market can be higher, while the total output in the market remains the same.

Next, consider point T (that is, a point to the left of point M). Here, firm A produces less than it does at point M and firm B produces more. In this case, we can see that the overall variable costs in the market increase by area UVI. This means that if the marginal cost of firm B exceeds that of firm A, the variable costs in the market can be higher while the market output remains the same by reducing firm B's output and increasing firm A's output by that amount.

In this way, in a competitive market where an environmental tax is in place, the level of output that each firm voluntarily chooses (point M) will consequently minimize the variable cost in the market. One advantage of environmental taxes is that they can minimize the variable (thus production) costs in the market by exploiting the profit-maximizing behavior of firms.

A major problem with environmental taxes may be the difficulty of determining the level of taxation to impose. To achieve the optimal outcome by using taxation, the policymaker needs to know the demand and supply curves of the market to choose an optimal level of tax to charge. However, given that only limited data is available, it is difficult to accurately estimate the shapes of the demand and supply curves of the market. In such a case, the policymaker need to choose the level of the tax based on limited information, and as a result, the tax may not be sufficient to achieve optimal targets set out in the policy goal.

2.2 Regulatory Instruments

Regulations can be classified into two types: concentration controls (e.g., vehicle emissions controls) and total amount control, that is, a regulation that limits the amount of pollutant emissions. Here we will consider total amount control. In essence, total amount control directly regulates the volume of emissions. The maximum amount of pollutant emissions also can be controlled indirectly by regulating the amount of production, as emissions depend crucially on production volume. Our discussion will focus on this indirect approach to regulating emissions. In particular, we will consider the case where the government implements total amount control by determining an optimal production volume, designating it as the maximum level of output in the entire market, and assigning individual firms the amount they can produce, so that the sum of their production volume equals the maximum level of output in the market. The advantage of this type of regulation is that the government can achieve the policy targets as long as the firms adhere to their allocated production volume.

When the government controls production volume, it is necessary to minimize the total cost of production in the market and thereby maximize social surplus. To do so, it needs to allocate production to firms in a way to equalize their marginal costs as at point M in Fig. 2.4. However, making such an allocation is difficult for several reasons. First, the government needs to accurately estimate the marginal cost curves for all firms, which is practically difficult given the limited sources of data and information. For this reason, misallocation, such as point N and point T in Fig. 2.5, may occur. If it does, the production (variable) cost of the market becomes greater; although the total volume of production in the market is controlled to the target level, the social surplus is not maximized.

Second, the government may exercise discretion in allocating the production. For example, if the government is influenced by the bargaining power of firms and/or takes into account the regulation's impact on the industries, the allocation will not be made to equate marginal costs across firms. It is likely that a larger amount of allocation is granted to large-sized firms with more bargaining power. In that case, social surplus decreases while the interests of some firms are protected. Furthermore, even if the government issues administrative guidance to firms that do not adhere to their quotas, they may not comply with it.

2.3 Tax or Subsidy?

At the beginning of this chapter, we mentioned that environmental taxes are preferable to subsidy schemes (i.e., subsidies on the reduction of production/pollution). This might sound odd because we demonstrated in Chap. 1 that it is possible to achieve the optimal level of output, minimize production costs, and maximize social surplus regardless of which instrument is used. It should be pointed out, however, that these are short-term results. In the long run, where firms enter the industry if they can earn an economic profit and exit the industry if they lose money, environmental taxes, and subsidies have different effects on firms' behaviors and the industry as a whole, as explained below.

The imposition of an environmental tax raises the costs of firms, thereby lowering the profit margins of those currently operating. This implies that firms, especially those that have not installed pollutant removal equipment or implemented energy-efficient technologies in production, must pay heavier environmental taxes and suffer from higher costs, and eventually will be forced to withdraw from the industry. Put another way, firms that remain in the industry will be exclusively those that adopt production systems to reduce energy and resource consumption. Accordingly, the whole industry will transition toward being more environmentally friendly. In addition, the industrial structure will also change: industries with large environmental impact will become relatively smaller than those with small environmental impact and conversely, industries with less environmental impact will grow relatively larger.

Contrastingly, a subsidy may make survival possible for firms that would have withdrawn from the industry in the case of an environmental tax. As a result, entries in the industry will be promoted. Industries that receive subsidies because of their high environmental impact will become relatively larger than industries with low environmental impact. Therefore, the transition to a low environmental impact society likely will be delayed.

In sum, an environmental tax and a subsidy have the same policy effect in the short term when no firm enters or exits from the industry. However, in the long term when entry and exit occur, an environmental tax differs from a subsidy in that the former induces the industry to lower its environmental impact while the latter does not. From a long-term perspective, therefore, an environmental tax is preferable to a subsidy in terms of its effects on the industrial structure.

The advantage of environmental tax comes with some cost, however. Specifically, the process of industrial adjustment may be accompanied by unemployment. When unemployment becomes a problem, governments may have to take measures to promote employment to achieve smooth industrial adjustment and the resulting transfer of labor between industries. It should also be noted that to mitigate unemployment and related social problems, a subsidy scheme may be effective to a certain extent. However, a subsidy should be provided only for a limited time and then replaced by an environmental tax after a certain transition period, given that a permanent subsidy scheme negatively impacts the long-term adjustment of the industry structure.

As a final remark, it should be mentioned that environmental taxes and subsidies also differ from the perspective of public finance. The introduction of an environmental tax will generate a new source of government revenues. Governments may use the increase in tax revenues to fund the tax cuts for existing indirect/income taxes, thereby mitigating the loss of social surplus in the goods and labor markets. On the other hand, subsidies are normally financed through income taxes and indirect taxes. Imposing indirect taxes on goods that do not incur external costs as well as income taxes, however, may lower social surplus in the goods and labor markets. For this reason, an environmental tax may have some advantage over a subsidy from a public finance point of view.

Box 2.1 Renewable Energy Policies and Challenges

The amount of renewable energy in Japan has increased since the introduction of the feed-in tariff (FIT) scheme in July 2012. It grew (at the end of FY2020) approximately four times higher since the implementation of the scheme. The FIT scheme requires electric utilities, such as Tokyo Electric Power Company (TEPCO), to purchase electricity generated from renewable energy sources at a higher rate than the normal electricity tariff. However, utilities are allowed to recover their purchase costs by increasing electricity prices. Thus, consumers bear the cost of renewable energy. The following are some of the challenges faced by renewable energy policies:

First, during periods of high solar generation due to long daylight hours or high wind generation due to strong winds, supply greatly exceeds consumption. Electric utilities are likely to reject purchase of the electricity from renewable energy generators to prevent damage to equipment caused by unbalanced demand and supply, resulting in a major power outage and the electricity generated must be discarded. This problem is more likely to occur in areas where renewable energy sources are concentrated. It is necessary to disperse the location of renewable energy generation areas and to promote the introduction of large storage batteries to solve this problem. Under a new policy scheme starting in FY2022, renewable energy producers that meet certain conditions will be required to switch to a Feed-in Premium (FIP) scheme, which is expected to give them an incentive to install large storage batteries. However, non-eligible renewable energy producers still have no incentive.

Second, solar panels contain hazardous chemicals and pose a risk of environmental pollution if abandoned or improperly disposed of after the power generation equipment is closed. Renewable energy generators may have incentives to abandon the equipment with no appropriate treatment or dispose of it with improper treatment to reduce the burden of disposal costs. A deposit system to cover disposal costs has been established since April 2022.

Finally, disaster risk, such as landslides and mudslides, increases during heavy rains, if photovoltaic power generation facilities are located in areas prone to disasters. However, no scheme, that discourages renewable energy generators to choose high-risk locations, has been introduced. Since April 2020, solar power plants with a capacity of 10 kW or more are required to purchase fire and earthquake insurance to cover the damage caused by natural disasters and earthquakes. This requirement is likely to promote the generators to choose lower risk locations. Because insurance premiums are higher in higher-risk locations. However, it is not legally binding and only implemented as a duty. Mandatory insurance should be considered.

Chapter 3
Property Right Approach and Emissions Trading Schemes

Toshi H. Arimura

Abstract The economist R. Coase observed that environmental problems can be resolved through bargaining between the affected parties as long as property rights, or rights to own or use the environment, were established. He also recognized that in many cases, transaction costs make bargaining difficult. This chapter first explains the Coase Theorem, property rights, and issues of transaction costs. We then extend the discussion by examining emissions trading, a policy instrument inspired by Coase's insight. We provide an economic explanation that demonstrates how the trading of pollution permits works as an efficient market-based instrument for reducing emissions.

Keywords The coase theorem · Property right approach · Transaction cost · Emissions trading · Cap and trade

3.1 Property Rights to the Environment

In Chaps. 1 and 2, we argued that environmental problems will not be resolved without government intervention and then discussed the advantages and disadvantages of the interventions such as subsidies and environmental taxes. In contrast to these arguments, Ronald Coase (1910–2013), a British-born American economist who earned the 1991 Nobel Prize in Economics, contends that environmental problems can be resolved without government intervention, as long as **property rights** (i.e., rights to own and use a good or resource) to use the environment are established (Coase 1960). If this theory, usually referred to as the Coase Theorem, holds true, then the role of government in managing environmental issues becomes a lot easier. Assigning property rights to all natural resources will be the sensible environmental policy.

In what follows, we will explain the Coase Theorem. In particular, we consider a situation where a factory belonging to a profit-maximizing firm produces air pollutants as by-products that are health hazards to local residents. We will then compare the outcomes across three different assignments of property rights: (1) no one holds

T. H. Arimura and A. Hibiki, *Introduction to Environmental Economics and Policy in Japan*, https://doi.org/10.1007/978-981-97-2187-0_3

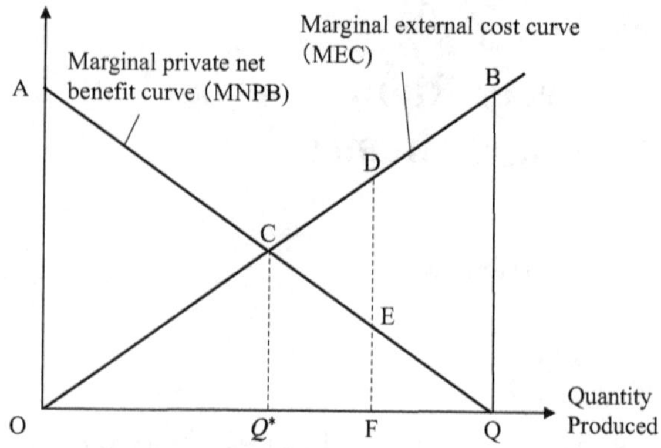

Fig. 3.1 Marginal external cost curve and marginal private benefit curve

property rights (i.e., the absence of property rights), (2) the rights are held by the residents in the polluted region, and (3) the rights are held by the polluting firm.

3.1.1 *The Model Setup*

Think about typical pollution problems, like the health hazards to local residents caused by factories' pollutants. For example, Yokkaichi Asthma, one of the four major pollution-caused diseases in Japan, occurred under very similar circumstances. In the city of Yokkaichi in Mie Prefecture, the incidence of asthma began increasing in the early 1960s. The main cause of the incidence was sulfur oxides and other pollutants emitted from petroleum complexes and other factories in the area (ERCA 1997).

As in the example, we consider a firm that produces air pollutants as by-products of production. For this firm, we assume that the more output is produced, the more profit is made, but at the same time, the amount of pollutants also increases. These relationships are succinctly expressed in Fig. 3.1; it illustrates how the private benefit (which is the firm's profits/surplus) and the cost of pollution damage vary across different levels of output by using the marginal private benefit (MPB) curve and the marginal external cost (MEC) curve, respectively.

3.1.2 *Marginal Private Benefit*

The **marginal private benefit** (**MPB**) is the additional profit the firm makes from producing one more unit of output; in other words, it is additional to the private benefit when an additional unit is produced. This means that the private benefit is the sum of private marginal benefits of the number of units produced. The marginal private benefit curve exhibits the relationship between the marginal private benefit and the level of output; the private benefit is therefore equal to the area under the **marginal private benefit curve**. For example, when the level of output is F (Q), the private benefit is represented as area OFEA (OQA).

The marginal private benefit curve is negatively sloped, reflecting that as production increases, the cost of production of one additional unit of output increases. For example, if an employee must work overtime or on holidays to increase production, the firm has to pay a higher rate of compensation to the employee. The cost of producing an additional unit becomes more expensive for the firm as the wage per unit of time increases.

The marginal private benefit curve tells us how much the firm produces in the absence of government intervention; the firm chooses to produce a quantity of Q, as it continues to operate until the incremental benefit from producing one more unit becomes zero. Below we will see, however, that Q is not a socially desirable level.

3.1.3 Marginal External Cost (MEC)

To identify the socially desirable level of output, it is not enough to look at the marginal private benefit curve alone; we also need to consider the external costs to society of pollutants caused by the firm's production. For example, in Yokkaichi, air pollutants emitted from petroleum complexes and other factories caused many people to suffer from chronic bronchitis, bronchial asthma, emphysema, and other health problems. Those who were severely affected by the pollution must have sacrificed their work and leisure time to attend to their health or be admitted to hospitals. Even for those who did not suffer much, the polluted air must have been unpleasant; in industrial cities in Japan in the 1960s, visibility was so poor due to sulfur oxides, soot and dust that one could not drive a car without turning on the headlights even during the day (ERCA 1997). Just like these examples, we assume that emissions caused by the firm's production are harmful to local residents (even if emissions do not cause health problems). We therefore consider the corresponding pollution damage as the external cost of the firm's production to society. We assume for simplicity that the amount of air pollutants is proportional to the level of output.

For analysis, all of the damage caused by the pollutants is translated into monetary terms. Then, the **marginal external cost** (MEC) is the additional external cost (i.e., the additional damage expressed in monetary terms) to society of the firm's producing one more unit of output. The marginal external cost curve in Fig. 3.1 exhibits how the marginal external cost is associated with the level of output. The marginal external cost curve is positively sloped, reflecting that the health hazards caused by one additional unit of emissions are often greater than those by the first unit of emissions.

The total external cost (i.e., the total amount of damage expressed in monetary terms) corresponds to the lower area of the marginal external cost curve. As you can see in the figure, the lower area increases as the output increases. For example, if the level of output is F, the magnitude of the damage is represented by area OFD; likewise, if the level of output is Q, the magnitude of the damage is represented by area OQB. This pattern reflects that an increase in production results in an increase in the amount of emissions and thus the damage.

3.1.4 *Absence of Property Rights*

We now consider the Coase Theorem by examining the outcome under three different assignments of property rights. We first examine the case when the property rights are not established, in other words, when the property rights are assigned to nobody. In this case, the level of output is determined by market equilibrium; accordingly, the firm chooses to produce a quantity of Q where the marginal private benefit is zero (i.e., the private benefit is the greatest), and the corresponding producer's surplus is represented by area OQA. It should be noted that this level of output results in the pollution damage where the external cost of production to society is represented by area OQB. If we define the social benefit to be the private benefit minus the external cost, it can be represented as "area OQA – area OQB" in the figure.

The market equilibrium in the absence of property rights is not desirable from society's vantage point. Suppose that the output is reduced from Q by a little. Then, the polluting firm's benefit is slightly reduced, but more than that, the pollution damage is reduced. In the aggregate, the social surplus has increased. Indeed, the social surplus can be made larger as long as the marginal external cost is larger in magnitude than the marginal private benefit. Put differently, the social surplus is greatest at the intersection of the marginal private cost curve and the marginal external cost curve, as represented by area OCA.

Some people may wonder how pollution damage is transformed into monetary terms. One way of doing so is based on how much monetary compensation people are willing to accept for the damage they experience. For some damage, however, people may be unwilling to accept monetary compensation, no matter how much it is. For example, one may contend that the damage of ozone depletion caused by chlorofluorocarbons should never have happened. In such a case, the magnitude of the damage is considered as infinite so that the marginal external cost curve is a vertical line through O. The two curves will then intersect at the zero production level, meaning that the socially desirable output becomes zero.

Box 3.1 Divers and the Fishery

Many divers come to the Okinawa Islands to enjoy the beautiful coral, but who owns the ocean they dive in? In fact, conflicts between local fishermen and diving companies over the use of the ocean can be problematic. Fishermen, who own fishing rights, claim that the divers who come to the islands violate their rights and demand nuisance fees from diving companies who bring in divers. Many companies have complied but some haven't. Who is right?

The right to fish is the right to make a living by fishing in a given body of water. If catches are reduced due to the presence of divers, it means that the divers violate the rights of fishermen and they need to compensate the damages. In this case, negotiations determine the number of divers, the catch, and the amount of compensation—the world that Ronald Coase envisioned will come true. However, if there is no evidence that divers caused a decrease in the catch, one can argue that diving companies have a reason for not paying the compensation. The problem lies partially with the fact that the right to fish is established while the right to dive is not.

3.1.5 *Maximizing Social Benefit Through Property Rights Assignments and Bargaining*

We have discussed a case where property rights to the environment (specifically property rights to the atmosphere in our discussion) are not explicitly defined. In such a case, pollution and environmental problems arise. Ronald Coase contends that the lack of clarity as to who owns the right to the environment is the cause of the problems. He also argues that once property rights are established, bargaining between polluters and victims will take place, leading to a socially desirable outcome.

3.1.6 *Property Rights Assigned to the Residents*

Consider the case where property rights are assigned to the residents (or the victims of pollution). It means, in our example, that the residents have the right to breathe clean air. The polluting firm infringes on that right and emits smoke, causing damage to the residents; the firm therefore must compensate for the damage. The residents then bargain with the firm to demand the compensation.

Suppose that the firm initially produced a quantity of Q, as in Fig. 3.1. As the residents own property rights, the firm must compensate them for the damage represented as area OQB. The compensation would obviously reduce the firm's profit and might even cause the firm to fall into the red. To reduce the burden of compensation, the firm therefore would consider reducing the quantity of output. Now, suppose that the output is reduced to a quantity of F. Then the profit will decrease by area FQE, but the amount of compensation will be reduced by area FQBD; the decrease in compensation is greater in magnitude than the profit lost. The burden on the firm will therefore be reduced if the level of output is reduced to F.

For the firm, it is in its best interest to further reduce its production volume; as long as the marginal external costs are greater than the marginal private benefits, the firm will be able to reduce the compensation burden. However, if the marginal external cost is less than the private marginal benefit (on the left side of Q* in the figure), the portion of the decline in profits will be larger than the reduced portion of the compensation. Therefore, there will be no reason for the firm to reduce its production to the level below Q*.

For residents, there is no reason to demand that the firm reduce production further than Q*. Even though the firm produces pollution, it provides equivalent monetary compensation as represented by area OQ*C. The level of residents' satisfaction with their lives is the same as it would be if there were no pollution damage at all (in other words, the external costs borne by the residents are zero) and the producer surplus of the firm is area OCA. In this case, the social surplus is maximized, and the socially desirable output is achieved.

3.1.7 Property Rights Assigned to the Polluter

Now let us consider the case where property rights are assigned to the polluting firm. In this case, the firm has been endorsed to pollute the atmosphere, so, moral issues aside, there would be no legal problem in producing emissions. Suppose, as before, that the firm initially produced Q in Fig. 3.1. Would the residents, who have no rights, be satisfied with the production Q? If the residents act rationally, they will begin to bargain with the firm to decrease its production. For example, if production is reduced to F, the firm's profits will be reduced by area FQE, but then the damage to the residents will be reduced by as much as area FQBD. If the residents compensate the firm's profits by the size of area FQE, the firm should have no objection to reducing its production to F. The residents pay the firm only for area FQE and obtain the utility of area FQBD (i.e., the damage is reduced), so they gain by the amount represented by area QBDE. In other words, the rational course of action for the residents would be to have the firm reduce its production and to compensate the firm for the lost profits.

Bargaining to reduce production and compensate for lost profits lasts until production becomes Q*. If production is reduced below a quantity of Q*, the reduction in damage is less than the benefit to be compensated. Hence, there is no incentive on the part of the residents to compensate the firm's profits. Here we see that the social surplus is maximized through bargaining even when the firm owns property rights. If the government is concerned with increasing social welfare, it does not need to worry about who to assign property rights to, as bargaining among the affected parties will solve that issue. It should be noted, however, that depending on who owns property rights, the incomes of the polluter and victims will vary (see Box 3.2).

Box 3.2 Determining Ownership and the Problems of Distribution

The Coase Theorem states that in solving environmental problems, it is important to establish the right to use the environment, and it does not matter who owns the right in the first place. Regardless of who has the right of use, negotiation solves the problem and maximizes the social benefits.

However, the distribution—who benefits and how much—depends largely on the determination of ownership rights. For example, what about giving rights to the polluter as in the example in this chapter? It is not socially acceptable for victims to compensate polluters. This is particularly so given that residents of the areas that suffer from factory pollutions are not necessarily wealthy. Pollution problems caused by nuisance facilities such as hazardous chemical plants and waste-related facilities in low-income neighborhoods are often reported in the United States as well. These issues have been discussed in terms of environmental justice in recent years. From the perspective of environmental justice, it would be appropriate to give the victim the right to use the environment in the case of pollution problems like the one discussed in this chapter.

3.2 Limitations of the Coase Theorem

3.2.1 Transaction Costs

So far, we have seen that under the Coase Theorem, once property rights are assigned, regardless of who owns the rights, a socially desirable outcome may be achieved through bargaining. Put differently, environmental problems persist because the affected parties cannot bargain with each other in the absence of property rights.

In practice, will the social surplus be maximized through bargaining as long as property rights are established? To answer this question, we need to consider **transaction costs**, that is, costs associated with bargaining. For example, victims of smoke emissions from a plant must spend a reasonable amount of time to bargain with the plant (e.g., take time off from work, cut back on household chores, and/or cut back on leisure time) to get to the negotiating table. Transaction costs also include fees and expenses to hire an attorney for the bargaining. All these transaction costs are not included in the marginal external costs because the external costs are the damage caused by smoke emissions, not the costs of bargaining.

Let us consider transaction costs in the case where property rights are assigned to the residents in the polluted region. If the residents' incremental utility from bargaining is smaller than the lost income due to taking time off from work, then bargaining is not likely to occur because there is no rationale for them to bargain. As such, pollution abatement may not occur, and the residents would have to put up with polluted air. Accordingly, the social surplus is not maximized even if the residents own property rights. Transaction costs can be significant for the victims of pollution damage, as exemplified by Yokkaichi asthma. The first spate of Yokkaichi asthma cases occurred in 1961, and the victims sued the polluters in 1967. In 1972, the district court ruled on the case. These intervening years lasted about ten years, and at the peak, the number of certified patients was 1,140 after 1970 (ERCA 1997).

Transaction costs of environmental problems tend to be expensive partly because the environment has a public good nature (See Box 1.1 in Chap. 1 for further discussion on this point), often making it difficult to estimate damage caused by them. While it may be possible to quantify health damages and missed income caused by air pollution, how can we accurately measure discomfort caused by pollution? In the absence of accurate estimates, individuals may have incentives to overreport the damage in order to receive more compensation than they are supposed to. Furthermore, theoretical studies suggest that this kind of self-interested behavior, if revealed to others, might lead to more people overreporting the damage they received, which may in turn result in breaking the bargaining. These consequences are attributed to the fact that the damage of environmental pollution is a negative public good and therefore shared by a number of individuals.

3.2.2 Problems with Identifying the Polluter for Bargaining

Another problem of the Coase Theorem lies in identifying the polluter for bargaining. For example, in an industrial area with many plants, it is difficult to identify which firm has caused environmental damages to which areas/residents and to what extent. This is especially the case with vehicle emissions, as exemplified by the Amagasaki air pollution lawsuit that resulted in settlement in 2000. In the lawsuit, the causes of pollution were identified as emissions not only from plants but also from vehicles, which means that the drivers were also considered as polluters.

In the case of drivers, identifying the sources of the damage and affected parties (i.e., whose cars have caused how much damage in which area) is even more difficult than in the case of plants. In addition, the impact of vehicle emissions on human health and the environment varies depending on so many conditions such as the level of congestion and time of a day the vehicle was used. Moreover, while it might be possible to identify the time and place of using a vehicle for business and commuting purposes, it is quite difficult to do so for private usages. If the relationship between polluters and victims is complicated as the case described above, victims will not know with whom they should bargain, and hence, the Coase Theorem does not hold.

This argument also applies to the issue of climate change. It is the current or previous generation who has been relying on fossil fuels such as oil and coal that have caused climate change. Nevertheless, the victims of climate change are the future generations and many of them are not even born. The victims are not on the negotiating table yet. One could argue that some of the **current generation** represent their interest in lieu of **future generations**. However, this does not mean that bargaining between the current and future generations is taking place in the way explicated by the Coase Theorem. Given that the majority of the current generation does not choose public transportation over private vehicles to mitigate the damage of climate change, it is clear that the social surplus is not maximized.

Note that the examples presented here is a classic example of air pollution. However, the idea of Coase's theorem can be established in many places for problems with externalities. For example, the construction of a high-rise building can deprive the surrounding residents of their right to light and generate negative externalities. The same argument holds true in such cases. If the residents of the affected neighborhood have the right to light, they can demand that the height of the building to be constructed be reduced. It can be expected that the outcome of the negotiations will settle on a socially desirable height.

Box 3.3 Tokyo Station and Air Rights

Coase's theorem is also applied in urban development in Japan. A case in point is the major renovation and earthquake retrofit on Tokyo Station. World War II air raids damaged and destroyed the roof and third floor of the building, reducing it to two stories. In commemoration of the station's 100th anniversary, it was decided in 2014 to restore the building to its original appearance and reinforce it against earthquakes. It turned out, however, that the restoration would cost around 50 billion JPY! To cover the high cost, Tokyo Station used air rights, putting the Coase's theorem into practice.

Floor area ratio (FAR) is the size of a building (or the maximum floor space) that is allowed to be constructed on a given piece of land. The Marunouchi area where Tokyo Station is located is permitted to construct high-rise buildings and designated as a special FAR district, meaning that buildings there can transfer or sell portions of unused FAR to other buildings. Instead of constructing a tall building, the station's owner (the East Japan Railway Company or JR East) sold its air rights to neighboring buildings and were able to raise the money to restore the historical building and make it earthquake proof.

3.3 Emissions Trading: Application of the Coase Theorem

A scheme that applies the Coase Theorem while treating the problem of transaction costs is **emissions trading**. In an emissions trading scheme (hereafter called "ETS"), property rights to the environment are permits to emit pollutants. With the aim of reducing not only emissions but also transaction costs, ETS has affected parties trade the allowances issued by government in the emissions market instead of having them bargain individually. Various ETSs have been adopted in countries and regions including the EU, U.S., Korea and China. An international ETS for greenhouse gas (GHG) emissions was proposed as a climate change measure in the Kyoto Protocol. The protocol was negotiated in 1997 and came into force in 2005 to establish international agreements to reduce GHG emissions cooperatively.

Let us take a closer look at how ETS works. Government first sets the acceptable level of GHG emissions in the economy. The target level is set based on various factors and is therefore not necessarily equal to the socially optimal level that the government aims to achieve by implementing environmental taxes. The government creates a permit, or the right to emit one unit of GHG emissions, issues permits only up to the total emissions limit that was set initially, and distribute the permits to firms. The amount of permits distributed to firms usually depends on their emissions levels in past years (**grandfathering**). As we will see later, the initial distribution will not influence the burden of ETS on the economy. Firms can then emit GHGs as much as their allowances permit. If they reduce emissions and have allowances to spare, they can opt to gain profit by selling them to other firms. Conversely, if their emissions level exceeds the allowances, they can buy additional allowances from others in the market to offset their emissions.

Governments should take initiative at the initial stages of establishing an allowance market, because firms are unfamiliar with the idea of property rights to produce emissions and thus may hesitate to buy and sell the rights. In addition, it is necessary for the government to monitor not only the approximate number of allowances held by each firm but also its emissions volume. Should firms emit more than their allowances, the government needs to enforce a penalty or fine on them. Otherwise, some firms may not comply with their allowances, which can result in a failure to achieve emissions reduction targets in the entire market.

3.3.1 ETS and Its Significance

Although it may sound unethical to trade property rights to pollute, ETS is a rational mechanism that aids firms into reducing their emissions in a cost-effective manner. Firms that can reduce emissions relatively cheaply will cut back their emissions. If reducing emissions is relatively costly, they will purchase allowances from the market. Consequently, the target level of emissions will be achieved at the lowest cost.

Let us consider the rationale for introducing ETS by using climate change measures as an example. Suppose that the world is composed of just two countries, A and B. Their CO_2 emissions demand curves are represented as Figs. 3.2 and 3.3. As explained in Chap. 1, the area under the demand curves represents utilities (that is, surplus) obtained from emitting CO_2. Emission reduction leads to smaller surplus. In the absence of regulations, the countries do not need to pay for their emissions and hence the price is 0. As a result, $E_A{}^0$ ($E_B{}^0$) is country A's (B's) CO_2 emissions. Total emissions in this world is $E_A{}^0 + E_B{}^0$.

The shape of the emissions demand curve is determined by a number of factors including the price of fossil fuels and the economic structure of the country. For this

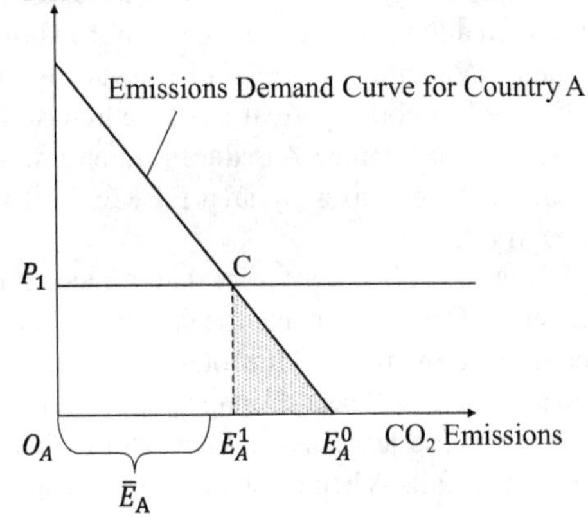

Fig. 3.2 Emissions demand curve for country A

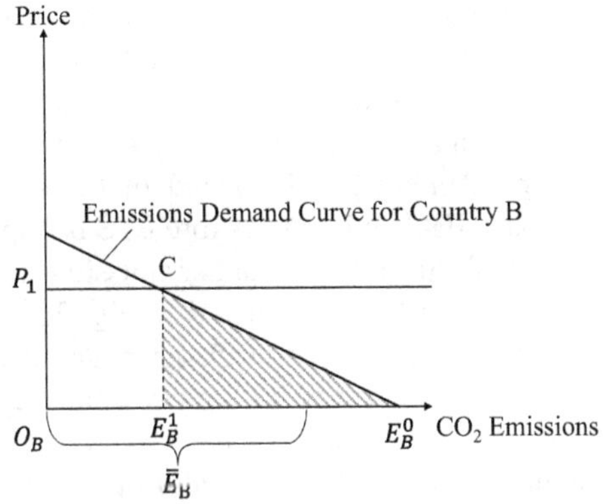

Fig. 3.3 Emissions demand curve for country B

reason, the emissions demand curves are likely to differ in shape across countries. Accordingly, we depict the figure in such a way that the slope of the demand curve differs between countries A and B. In particular, country A's slope is steeper than that of country B, indicating that the cost of reducing emissions is greater in country A than in country B. As a real-world example, Japan has made various investments in energy conservation through the two oil crises of the 1970s and the nation's energy consumption per unit of GDP (gross domestic product) is already lower than that of other developed countries. This made it more difficult for Japan to reduce its carbon dioxide emissions than other industrialized countries. In other words, the cost of reducing emissions was relatively high in Japan when Kyoto Protocol entered into force in 2005 Japan's situation then is similar to that of country A in our example.

To reduce emissions in the world, suppose that ETS is introduced with the goal of setting the total global emissions as $\bar{E}$. In this case, allowances are set based on the total emissions targets and allocated to both countries. Suppose that country A is allocated with $\bar{E}_A$.

Under the ETS, once their allowances are allocated, countries A and B can buy and sell their allowances. For example, if the allowance price is P_1, then it is reasonable for country A to emit $E_A{}^1$ worth of allowances. Since this amount exceeds the allowances allocated to country A, it has to purchase allowances from country B. Now, let's assume that country A reduces its emissions to $E_A{}^1$. The surplus (or income) of country A decreases by area $E_0ACE_A{}^1$. This is the cost of reducing emissions in country A.

How is an allowance price determined? If the price is P_1, then emissions in country B is $E_B{}^1$. Country B makes decisions about buying and selling allowances, just like in country A. In this case, the total emissions are $E_A{}^1 + E_B{}^1$. If the emissions are greater than $\bar{E}$, there will be a shortage of allowances and the allowance price will rise. If the emissions are less than $\bar{E}$, there will be a surplus of allowances and the allowance price will fall. When these adjustments are made and when the total emissions and the emissions targets are aligned, the demand and supply of emissions will balance with each other. This is how emissions trading works.

By using the demand curves for both countries, we can see the level at which the allowance price is determined in the market in more detail. We reverse the left and right sides of the demand curve for country B, as if it were mirrored, and combine that figure with the figure for country A. Let us fit the vertices of the triangle together as illustrated in Fig. 3.4. The length of the two ends of the figure (i.e., O_AO_B) represents the total GHG emissions before ETS is implemented.

To make the total amount of emissions $\bar{E}$ means that the width of this entire figure is reduced to $\bar{E}$, as illustrated in Fig. 3.5. In this case, the demand and supply of allowances balance with each other at price P* (i.e., the height of the intersection (G) of the demand curves for the two countries). At this price, the quantity demanded by country A (country B) is $E_A{}^*$ ($E_B{}^*$). The total quantities demanded by the two countries are equal to the width of Fig. 3.5, i.e., $\bar{E}$. If the price is higher than P*, the price falls because the demand is less than the supply, and vice versa, and an equilibrium price P* is expected to be realized.

If the initial allocation for country A is $\bar{E}_A$, then the country will purchase allowances from country B for the amount of $E_A{}^* - \bar{E}_A$. Since the total emissions

Fig. 3.4 Emissions demand curve before the adoption of ETS

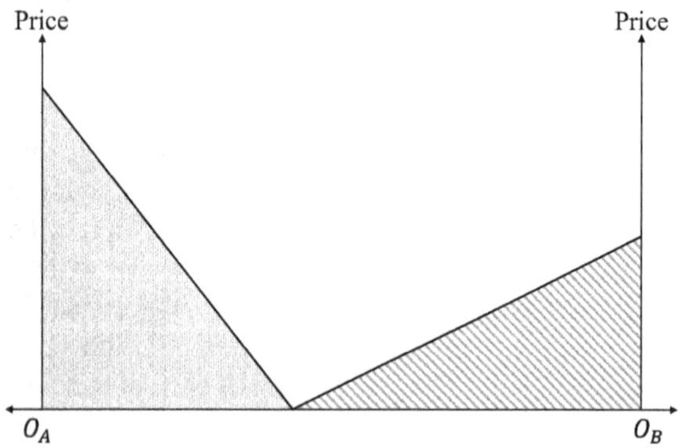

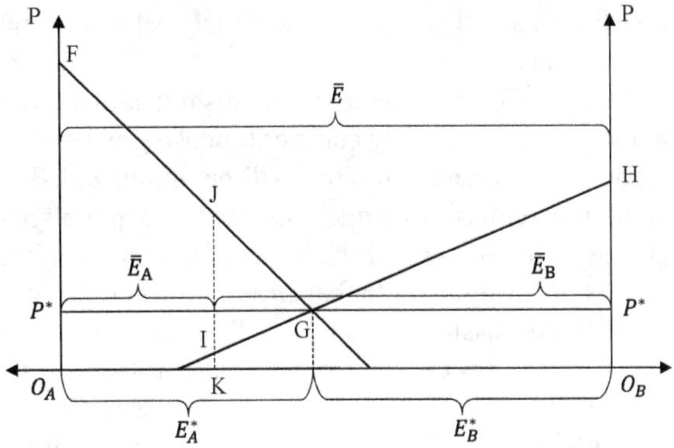

Fig. 3.5 Emissions demand curve after the adoption of ETS

target is $\bar{E}$, the initial allocation for country B is $\bar{E}_B = \bar{E} - \bar{E}_A$. In this case, if the price is P*, country B is willing to sell only $\bar{E}_B - E_B^*$ of its allowances. Here, the supply and demand for allowances balance each other.

Let us look at the transactions of allowances in terms of the cost to each country to reduce its emissions. The sale of allowances by country B means that it will be able to emit less and therefore must reduce its emissions. Doing so is relatively easy for country B because the abatement cost is less for country B than for country A. Country A, where abatement cost is high, does not need to reduce emissions by the amount of allowances purchased from country B. This is a very rational scheme for the world economy as a whole. As a result of emissions trading, country B, where emissions reduction is relatively cheaper, cuts down its emissions by a larger amount; country A, where emissions reduction is more costly, decreases emissions by a smaller amount.

Now, let's consider the total cost of reducing emissions by using Fig. 3.5. In the case where countries A and B trade allowances, emissions produced by country A are E_A^* and by country B are E_B^*, so the total surplus is area O_AFGHO_B. What happens if they do not trade allowances but match their emissions level to the number of allowances initially held? In that case, countries A and B are allowed to emit $\bar{E}$A and $\bar{E}_B$, respectively. This is a case similar to the scheme proposed in the Kyoto Protocol, in which emissions targets for developed countries have been determined but allowance trading between countries is not accepted. In this case, the surplus for country A is area O_AFJK and for country B is area O_BHIK, which means that the total surplus is reduced by area JGI. By comparison, we can see that the countries can minimize the total abatement costs by adopting ETS and trading their allowances.

It should be noted that the allowance allocation to countries (i.e., how much allocation is granted to which country) does not affect the abatement costs in the world economy. This is the same logic as in the Coase Theorem that the way in which property rights are allocated does not affect the outcome of bargaining. Nonetheless, the way in which the initial allocation is made will affect which country benefits and how much, and therefore, the adjustments between the affected parties on the initial allocation is not easy.

In sum, ETS is a market mechanism that incentivizes countries where emissions reductions are relatively cheaper to make greater reductions. As a result, the global burden of reducing emissions will be minimized. The money that was supposed to be used on emissions reductions can be spent on something else for more effective purposes. In this sense, ETS is an efficient market-based instrument.

It is important to note that emissions trading is often used as a domestic system. The first successful example of ETS is SO_2 allowance market in U.S. It was introduced to address the issue of acid rain problem and regulated SO_2 emissions from fossil fuel power plants. As we will discuss in Chap. 9, many countries and regions now implement ETS as a major policy instrument to mitigate CO_2 emissions from industries and power plants.

Box 3.4 Marginal Abatement Cost

Environmental economics frequently employs the concept of **marginal abatement costs**, which is useful for understanding the mechanisms of emissions trading. Marginal abatement costs are the additional costs required to reduce emissions by one unit. Initially, costs are low due to easy reduction options such as energy efficiency improvement through heat conservation. However, as the emissions reduction progresses, easy options diminish and additional costs increase. One example includes R&D expenditures or equipment investment to implement new industrial processes. Thus, a marginal abatement cost curve can be drawn with emission reductions on the horizontal axis and marginal abatement costs on the vertical axis. The curve then rises to the right.

The case study on emissions trading in this chapter can also be understood by examining the marginal abatement costs for each country. Marginal abatement costs of two countries become equal through the price of emission allowances, resulting in efficient emissions reduction. In the case of an environmental tax, emissions are reduced to a level at which the marginal abatement cost is equal to the environmental tax.

Many studies on climate change countermeasures have used the marginal abatement cost curve.

3.3.2 Transaction Costs in ETS

While emissions trading is an idea inspired by the Coase Theorem, it does not envision bargaining between polluters and victims. By design, the scheme has given up on the idea of maximizing social surplus by bargaining between the two sides. Under the scheme, the government sets the total allowances, and a certain amount of emissions will be reduced at a minimal cost by having polluters trade their allowances. This avoids the problem of transaction costs, i.e., what hinders bargaining between victims and perpetrators, and facilitates trading between polluters.

In practice, when adopting ETS, governments may have to facilitate the setup of the market to prevent the cost of transactions from becoming too great. It has been observed that after a certain period of time, the cost of trading declines and polluters will be able to trade allowances smoothly. As long as transaction costs are taken into account, ETS can be an effective solution, particularly for environmental problems in which a large number of polluters are involved.

3.3.3 ETS and Environmental Tax

It is also worth noting the relationship between emissions trading and environmental taxes, as both are price-based systems that efficiently reduce emissions of pollutants or greenhouse gases. Both policy instruments are expected to have similar effects in terms of economic efficiency. It is important to note that while the two policy instruments may have similar economic effects, they differ in their ability to achieve environmental objectives. If both countries were to implement an environmental tax at P*, they would achieve the same level of emission reductions under ETS in this example.

However, in practice, the two policy instruments have different characteristics in terms of achieving environmental goals. Emissions trading ensures that emission reduction targets are met, while a tax makes it difficult to predict the amount of emission reductions in advance. Additionally, environmental taxes and emissions trading have distinct effects and implications in cases of uncertainty regarding the emission demand curve and marginal abatement costs. Chapter 4 addresses this topic.

References

Coase, R. (1960) "The Problem of Social Cost", The Journal of Law and Economics. Vol. 3 (1–44)

ERCA (Environmental Restoration and Conservation Agency) (1997) Japan's Experience of Air Pollution: Challenge to the Sustainable Development. Kogai Kenko Higai Hosho Yobo Kyokai

Chapter 4
Uncertainty and Policy Choice: Carbon Tax or Emissions Trading Scheme

Akira Hibiki

Abstract As we explained in Chaps. 1 and 3, regulations, taxation, or any policy instruments could maximize social surplus if policymakers have perfect information about the demand curve, supply curve, and marginal external cost curve. In reality, however, governments do not have perfect information and therefore can mistakenly determine the optimal level of production, emissions, or an environmental tax, resulting in a decrease in social surplus. In this chapter, we consider which policy option is desirable—environmental taxes (we take a carbon tax as an example) or emissions trading schemes—to mitigate a decrease in social surplus in the presence of uncertainty due to imperfect information.

Keywords Carbon tax · Emissions trading scheme · Permits · Uncertainty

Chapters 1 and 3 explained that it is possible to abate CO_2 emissions to an optimal level either by an environmental tax (or a carbon tax) or an emissions trading scheme, and that the level of the tax and the price of the permit will equal at the optimal abatement/emissions level. In Chaps. 1 and 3, it is assumed that the government knows the optimal emissions level and thus optimally sets the level of the tax or the number of permits to issue because it has perfect information regarding the CO_2 demand and marginal external costs thereby identifying these functions correctly.

In reality, however, governments do not have perfect information and therefore have to predict the functions based on imperfect information and make decisions accordingly. In this chapter, we examine which type of measure is best suited in the presence of uncertainty due to imperfect information. In particular, we consider policy instruments that control prices (e.g., a carbon tax) or quantities (e.g., an emissions trading scheme) in terms of efficiency in resource allocation.[1]

---

[1] This section is written based on Yohe (1976). A comparison of command-and-control and environmental taxes under uncertainty is made in Weitzman (1974).

T. H. Arimura and A. Hibiki, *Introduction to Environmental Economics and Policy in Japan*, https://doi.org/10.1007/978-981-97-2187-0_4

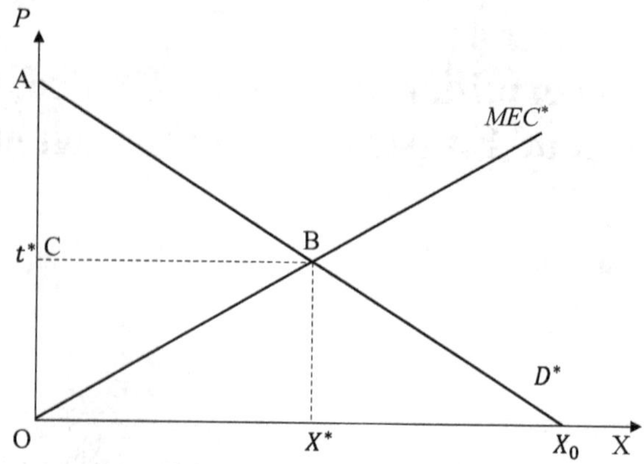

Fig. 4.1 Optimal carbon tax under perfect information

4.1 Policy Choice and Total Social Surplus Under Perfect Information

Before addressing the issue of uncertainty caused by imperfect information, we review the outcomes of implementing a carbon tax and an emissions trading scheme when the government has perfect information. We start with the case of implementing a carbon tax. Figure 4.1 shows the CO_2 demand curve (D^*) and the marginal external cost curve (MEC^*), with CO_2 price[2] (P) on the vertical axis and the amount of CO_2 emissions (X) on the horizontal axis.

As shown in the figure, social surplus is maximized at point B and the optimal level of emissions is X^*. When the government does not implement any environmental measure, CO_2 price is equal to zero and CO_2 will be emitted up to X_0. The optimal level of the tax to reduce emissions to X^* is t^*. In this case, the consumer surplus (CS^*) of carbon emissions, the revenue raised by the tax (T^*), and the external cost (EC^*) would be

$$CS^* = \text{area ABC},\ T^* = \text{area OCBX}^*,\ EC^* = \text{area OBX}^*$$

Thus the social surplus (SS^*) would be

$$SS^* = CS^* + T^* - EC^* = \text{area OAB}$$

By using Fig. 4.2, let's consider the case the government adopts an emissions trading scheme. To achieve the emissions level X*, the government needs to issue X* units of permits that allow one unit of emissions per permit. We assume that this is an auction type system meaning that there is no initial allocation of the permits to each firm.

---

[2] Under the carbon taxation, the carbon price indicates a carbon tax. Under an emissions trading scheme, the carbon price indicates the price of permits as is explained later.

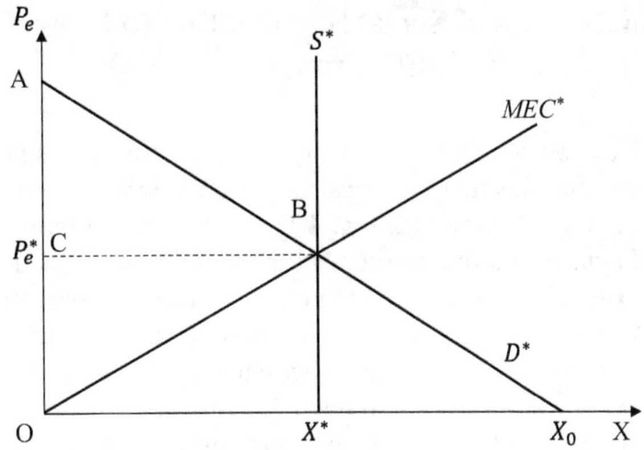

Fig. 4.2 Emissions trading scheme under perfect information

Figure 4.2 is similar to Fig. 4.1, but it shows a demand curve for *emissions permits* (D^*) and the marginal external cost curve (MEC^*) with the price of the permits (P_e) on the vertical axis and the quantity of the permits (X) on the horizontal axis. S^* is the permit supply curve. A firm must own one permit for one unit of CO_2 emissions, so the demand for one unit of emissions corresponds to the demand for one permit. Therefore, the demand price of the permit equals that of CO_2, and accordingly, the permit demand curve in Fig. 4.2 is identical to the CO_2 demand curve in Fig. 4.1. In a similar vein, the marginal external cost curve in Fig. 4.2 is identical to that in Fig. 4.1.

As shown in Fig. 4.2, the supply of and the demand for the permits are in equilibrium at point B. The equilibrium price of the permits is P_e^*. The consumer surplus (CS_e^*), the revenues from the sale of the permits (T_e^*), and the external cost (EC_e^*) are

$$CS_e^* = \text{area ABC},\ T_e^* = \text{area OCBX}^*,\ EC_e^* = \text{area OBX}^*$$

Thus the social surplus (SS_e^*) is

$$SS_e^* = CS_e^* + T_e^* - EC_e^* = \text{area OAB}$$

By comparing the surpluses in Figs. 4.1 and 4.2, we obtain:

$$CS_e^* = CS^*,\ T_e^* = T^*,\ EC_e^* = EC^*,\ SS_e^* = SS^*$$

Also, it is clear that the level of the carbon tax and the price of the permits are the same:

$$t^* = P_e^*$$

4.2 Loss of Social Surplus Due to Imperfect Information on the MEC Curve

Now we consider a case where the government has perfect information on the CO_2 demand function and *imperfect* information on the marginal external cost function. Figure 4.3 resembles Fig. 4.1, but the only difference is that Fig. 4.3 has MEC^1. Suppose that the government incorrectly estimates that MEC^1 is the true marginal external cost curve and therefore mistakenly considers that the optimal amount of CO_2 emissions is X^1 to maximize the predicted social surplus.

Suppose also that the government imposes a carbon tax and sets the level of the tax to t^1 to abate emissions to X^1. In this case, the consumer surplus (CS^1), the carbon tax revenue (T^1), and the external cost (EC^1) will be

$$CS^1 = \text{area AFE},\ T^1 = \text{area OFEX}^1,\ EC^1 = \text{area OGX}^1$$

Thus, the total social surplus (SS^1) is

$$SS^1 = CS^1 + T^1 - EC^1 = \text{area OAEG}$$

and the loss of the social surplus (ΔSS^1) due to the imperfect information is

$$\Delta SS^1 = SS^1 - SS^* = \text{area BEG}$$

Next, we examine the case in which the government introduces an emissions trading scheme to achieve the same emissions level (X^1). For this purpose, the government should issue X^1 units of permits. The CO_2 demand function in Fig. 4.3 can be interpreted as the demand curve for the permits just like the one in Fig. 4.2, if the CO_2 price (the quantity of emissions) on the vertical (horizontal) axis is replaced with the permit price (the quantity of the permits supplied/demanded). S^1 represents the supply curve for the permits. We can see that at point E, the equilibrium price

Fig. 4.3 Loss of surplus due to imperfect information on external costs

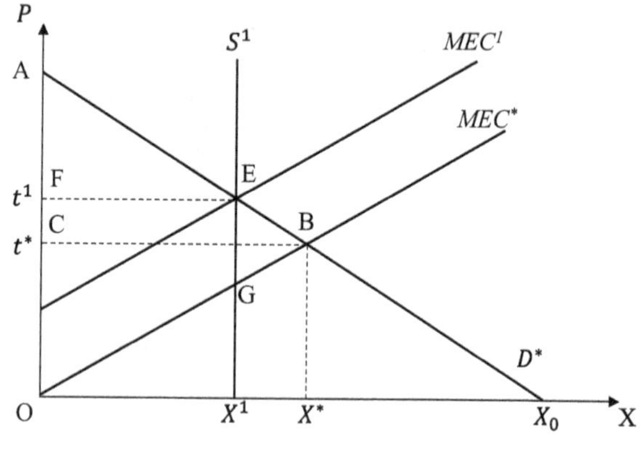

of the permit is t^1, i.e., identical to the case when the carbon tax is adopted. The consumer surplus ($CS_e{}^1$), the revenue from the permit sales ($T_e{}^1$) and the external cost ($EC_e{}^1$) are

$$CS_e^1 = \text{area AFE}, T_e^1 = \text{area OFEX}^1, EC_e^1 = \text{area OGX}^1$$

Hence, the social surplus ($SS_e{}^1$) is

$$SS_e^1 = CS_e^1 + T_e^1 - EC_e^1 = \text{area OAEG}$$

and the loss of the social surplus ($\Delta SS_e{}^1$) due to the imperfect information is

$$\Delta SS_e^1 = SS_e^* - SS_e^1 = \text{area BEG}$$

As shown above,

$$\Delta SS^1 = \Delta SS_e^1$$

In sum, when the government has imperfect information on the marginal external cost function, the loss of the social surplus would be the same regardless of whether a carbon tax or an emissions trading scheme is implemented.

4.3 Loss of the Social Surplus Due to Imperfect Information on the CO_2 Demand Function

Next, we consider a case where the government has perfect information on the marginal external cost function and imperfect information on the CO_2 demand function. This is the case where the government incorrectly estimates that D^2 is the true CO_2 demand function, as shown in Fig. 4.4 (i.e., Fig. 4.1 plus D^2). Here, the government mistakenly assumes that the optimal amount of emissions is X^2.

Suppose a carbon tax is introduced to abate emissions to X^2. Then the level of the tax set by the government would be t^2 to maximize the predicted social surplus. Because the true CO_2 demand function is D*, the emissions level is X^3. Therefore, the consumer surplus (CS^2), the carbon tax revenue (T^2), and the external costs (EC^2) are

$$CS^2 = \text{araeAGE}, T^2 = \text{area OEGX}^3, EC^2 = \text{areaOHX}^3$$

The social surplus (SS^2) is

$$SS^2 = CS^2 + T^2 - EC^2 = \text{area OAGH}$$

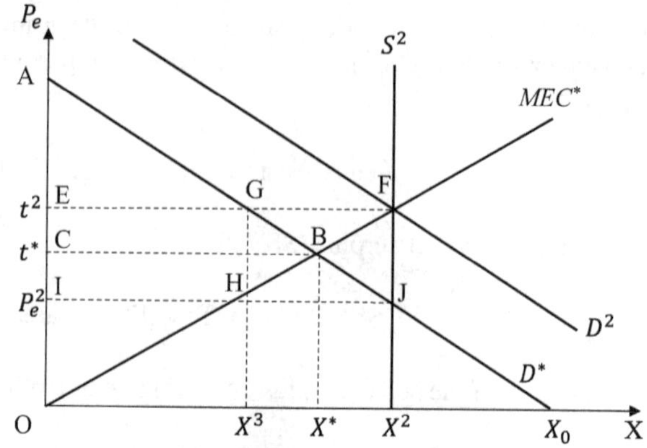

Fig. 4.4 Loss of the social surplus due to imperfect information on CO_2 demand curve

and the loss of the social surplus (ΔSS^2) due to the imperfect information is

$$\Delta SS^2 = SS^* - SS^2 = \text{area BEH}$$

If an emissions trading scheme is chosen to achieve the same emissions level, the government issues X^2 permits. As in Fig. 4.3, the CO_2 demand function in Fig. 4.4 can be interpreted as the permit demand curve if the CO_2 price (the quantity of emissions) on the vertical (horizontal) axis is replaced with the permit price (the quantity of the permits supplied/demanded). S^2 represents the supply curve for the permits just like S^1 in Fig. 4.3. The equilibrium price of the permit is $P_e{}^2$ at point F. The consumer surplus ($CS_e{}^2$), the revenue from the sale of the permits ($T_e{}^2$), and the external cost (EC_e^2) are

$$CS_e^2 = \text{arae} AIJ, \; T_e^2 = \text{area } OIJX^2, \; EC_e^2 = \text{area } OFX^2$$

The social surplus ($SS_e{}^2$) is

$$SS_e^2 = CS_e^2 + T_e^2 + EC_e^2 = \text{area OAB} - \text{area BFJ}$$

and the loss of the social surplus (ΔSS_e^2) in the absence of perfect information is

$$\Delta SS_e^2 = SS_e^2 - SS_e^* = \text{area BFJ}$$

4.4 Loss of the Social Surplus: The Slopes of the MEC Curve and the CO_2 Demand Curve

The relationship between ΔSS^2 and ΔSS_e^2 depends on the slopes of the marginal external cost curve and the CO_2 demand curve. We examine how the loss of the social surplus changes in accordance with the shapes of these curves. We start with the marginal external cost curve.

(1) The MEC Curve and the Loss of Total Social Surplus

To examine how the size of the surplus loss varies with the slopes of the marginal external cost curve, we compare the difference between the loss incurred by adopting a carbon tax and the loss incurred by implementing an emissions trading scheme when the marginal external cost curve is MEC* and MEC**, respectively, as shown in Fig. 4.5.

We first consider the case where a carbon tax is chosen over an emissions trading scheme. As discussed above, if the marginal external cost curve is MEC^*, the social

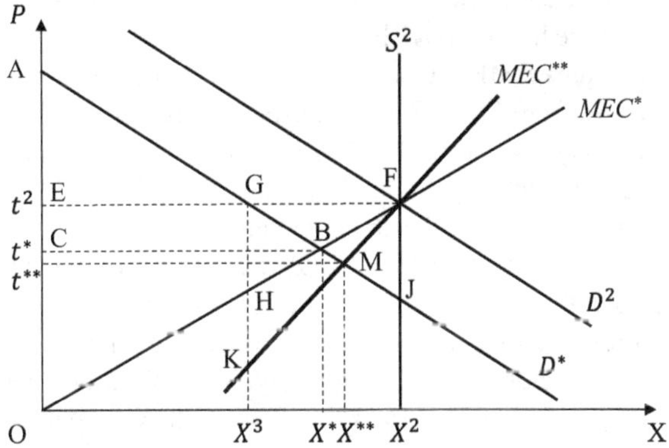

Fig. 4.5 MEC curves and loss of total social surplus

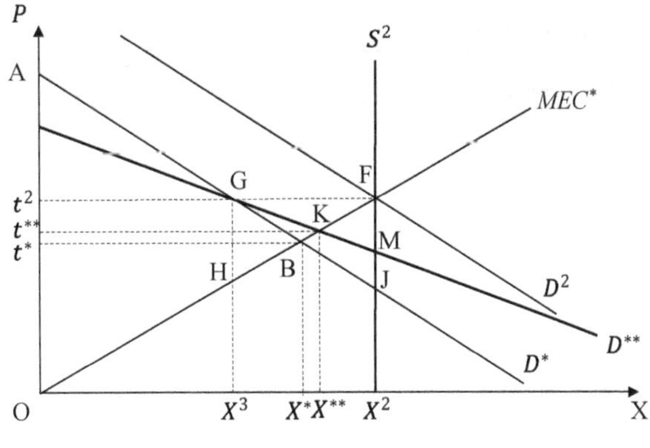

Fig. 4.6 CO_2 demand curves and loss of total social surplus

surplus loss caused by the government incorrectly estimating that D^2 is the true CO_2 demand function is area BGH. Similarly, the loss that occurs when the curve is MEC^{**} is area MGK. Since area MGK > area BGH, the steeper the slope of the curve, the greater the loss. Next, let's consider the case where an emissions trading scheme is adopted instead of a carbon tax. If the curve is MEC^*, the social surplus loss is area BFJ. Likewise, if it is MEC^{**}, the loss is area MFJ. Since area BFJ > area MFJ, the steeper the curve, the smaller the loss.

(2) The CO_2 Demand Curve and the Loss of Total Social Surplus

We now turn to the CO_2 demand curve and examine how the shape of the curve affects the size of the loss in the social surplus. Similar to what we did in 1), we compare the difference between the loss incurred by having a carbon tax imposed and that by having an emissions trading scheme implemented when the CO_2 demand curve is D^* and D^{**}. First, we examine the case where a carbon tax is adopted. As we have seen, if the CO_2 demand curve is D^*, the loss caused by the government incorrectly assuming D^2 as the true CO_2 demand curve is area BGH. Similarly, the loss that occurs when the demand curve is D^{**} is area KGH. Since area KGH > area BGH, the flatter the curve, the larger the loss.

In the case where an emissions trading scheme is chosen, if the CO_2 demand curve is D^*, the loss is area BFJ. Similarly, the loss is area KMF if the demand curve is D^{**}. Since area KMF < area BFJ, the flatter the curve, the smaller the loss in surplus. As we can see from Fig. 4.7, if the absolute value of the slope of the marginal external cost curve equals that of the CO_2 demand curve, then the loss from the carbon taxation equals the loss by the implementation of an emissions trading scheme.

To conclude, if the absolute value of the slope of the marginal external cost curve is *greater* than that of the CO_2 demand curve, the surplus loss from the taxation is greater than the loss from the adoption of an emissions trading scheme. In this case, it is desirable to choose an emissions trading scheme over a carbon tax to minimize the loss in social surplus. Conversely, if the absolute value of the slope of the marginal external cost curve is *less* than that of the CO_2 demand curve, the loss arising from choosing an emissions trading scheme is greater than the loss arising from choosing

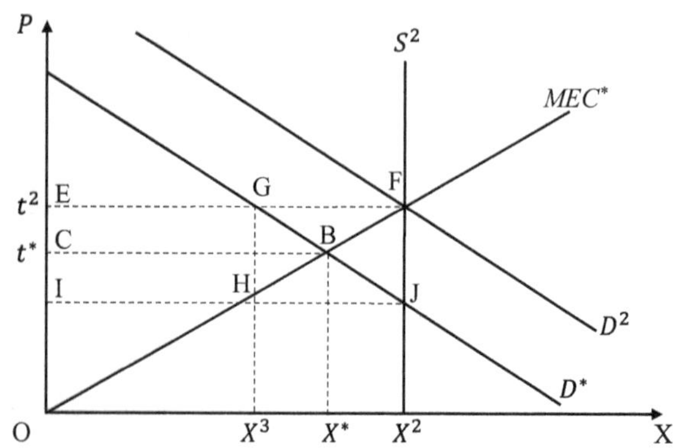

Fig. 4.7 Equivalence of carbon tax and emissions trading scheme

a carbon tax. Therefore, it is desirable to choose a carbon tax over an emissions trading scheme.

Box 4.1 Climate Adaptation Measures: Making Agriculture More Resilient to Climate Change Risks

Climate change has significantly impacted agriculture and food production. For example, rising temperatures lower crop yields in high-temperature regions and increase yields in colder regions. More frequent and intense hurricanes cause more severe flooding which results in reduced crop production. Strategies and actions to mitigate the impacts of climate change are adaptation measures. Agricultural adaptation practices include the development of crop varieties resistant to extreme temperatures and switching to crops that thrive at high temperatures.

While the average annual temperature has been increasing, temperatures and precipitation fluctuate every year. Some years have high temperatures and heavy rainfall, while others experience low temperatures and little rain. Agricultural yields may suffer from high temperatures in the previous year and flood damage this year, or may not suffer any significant damage at all in a different year. If the temperature increase is greater than the projected increase, farmers who choose crops that match the projection will suffer reduced yields. Similarly, if the temperature is lower than the projection, farmers who choose crops that match the projection may lose profits due to inappropriate crop choices. Thus, short-term weather fluctuations cause yield and damage fluctuations.

Mitigating these damage or risk fluctuations is an integral part of the adaptation measures. For example, the diversification of cultivation areas reduces risks. Likewise, growing crops that suit various temperatures, such as planting high and moderate-temperature-tolerant crops, reduces the risk of income fluctuations for farmers. Cultivating crops at different times of the year is also effective in reducing climate risks such as high temperatures and flooding. However, these practices are more feasible for large-scale farmers, but not for small-scale farmers.

Smart agricultural technologies, such as robotics and ICT, can also mitigate climate risks. However, larger-scale and younger farmers are more likely to be engaged in smart farming as small-scale farmers are not likely to afford fixed costs associated with technology and equipment, and it may be challenging for aging farmers to learn the skills necessary for smart farming. In addition, the benefits of acquiring hard-won skills and technology are small if they have no successors. Thus, those farmers are not likely to be engage in them.

These are the challenges that farmers in Japan face today. The majority of Japanese farmers are small-scale, part-time, and aging farmers with few successors. The entry of large-scale farmers must be encouraged to increase agricultural profitability and influence younger generations to enter the farming industry. It will also reduce the number of part-time farmers. Establishing institutional mechanisms that guide the industry to reduce risks and facilitate farmers' adoption of climate-smart practices is also important.

Cooperation among farmers is also the key to effective agriculture adaptation. Farmers, including those located in different regions, can cooperate to increase crop diversity across locations and to reduce their income risk by sharing total income. Nearby farmers can adopt smart farming, if they can establish a cooperative structure to share the devices and facilities for smart farming. As a collaborative farming group, they can also utilize financial instruments such as weather derivatives and disaster insurance. If insurance companies offer group policies with reduced premiums (or if the government subsidizes policy premiums), small farmers gain better access to these climate-adaptive instruments as part of their adaptation measures.

References

Weitzman, M. (1974) "Prices vs. Quantities", The Review of Economic Studies, Vol. 41, Issue 4, pp. 477–491. https://doi.org/10.2307/2296698

Yohe, G. (1976) "Substitution and the Control of Pollution--A Comparison of Effluent Charges and Quantity Standards Under Uncertainty", Journal of Environmental Economics and Management, Vol. 3, Issue 4, pp. 312–324. https://doi.org/10.1016/0095-0696(76)90003-6

Chapter 5
Waste Management: Optimal Disposal Fee and Intergenerational Use of the Landfill

Akira Hibiki

Abstract The amount of solid waste increases with economic growth, which results in decreasing the remaining capacity of landfills. Because landfill space is not unlimited and the construction of new sites is often difficult due to the "not in my backyard" (NIMBY) syndrome and various constraints, an overabundance of waste produced by the current generation causes a shortage of landfills for future generations. In this chapter, we consider the optimal intergenerational use of landfills and optimal disposal fee policy that maximizes the sum of the social surpluses of those generations.

Keywords Solid waste · Waste management · Optimal intergenerational use of landfills · Disposal fee · Unit pricing

The amount of solid waste increases with the economic growth and decreases the remaining capacity of the landfill. The landfill is considered as the NIMBY (not in my backyard) facility, which is not easy to construct. If the waste generation of the present generation is excessive, future generations will not be able to use the sufficient landfill. Therefore, it is important to consider the optimal use of landfill sites between current and future generations to maximize the sum of the social surpluses of those generations.

The disposal fees on waste generators are expected to reduce solid waste generation. In this chapter, we will examine how effective the disposal fees on waste generators are in reducing the optimal level of generation to maximize the sum of the social surpluses of current and future generations. For this purpose, we will compare outcomes under three different policies: (1) no disposal fee is imposed on generators, (2) a flat fee is imposed, and (3) a fee per unit of waste emissions (i.e. unit-pricing) is imposed and examine the optimal policy condition to achieve the optimal waste generation (i.e. optimal use of the landfill) of the current and future generations.

T. H. Arimura and A. Hibiki, *Introduction to Environmental Economics and Policy in Japan*, https://doi.org/10.1007/978-981-97-2187-0_5

5.1 Economic Analysis of Waste Disposal Charges

To simplify our analysis, this section will focus on solid waste that is produced and disposed of by the current generation. Waste management practices from an intergenerational perspective will be discussed in the next section where we consider optimal pricing schemes for both the current and future generations.

5.1.1 The Model Setup

Figure 5.1 illustrates the demand of waste generators (i.e., households) for disposal services (D) and the marginal cost of disposal to the municipality (MC). In the figure, the horizontal axis represents the amount of waste and the vertical axis represents the disposal fee per unit of waste charged to households (as well as the marginal cost of disposal service to the municipality, i.e., the incremental cost to the municipality of disposing of one additional unit of waste). Because households receive the services in accordance with the amount of waste they generate, the demand is expressed in terms of the amount of waste that households want to generate. The demand curve slopes downward to the right, reflecting that as the disposal fee becomes higher, households will generate less waste by putting more effort into waste management practices (e.g., avoiding disposable products and refusing packaging). It should be also noted that as the demand curve represents the marginal utility (cf. Chap. 1), the demand curve for disposal services corresponds to the households' marginal utility from generating waste (i.e., the incremental utility from generating one additional unit of waste).

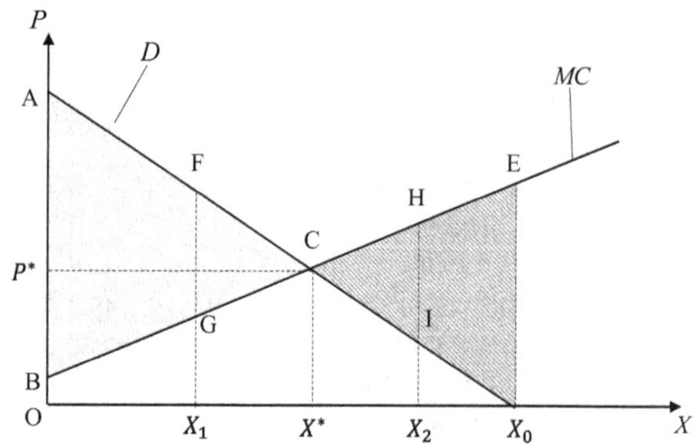

Fig. 5.1 Waste disposal and disposal fees

5.1.2 Optimal Amount of Waste

Households generate and dispose of waste as a result of consuming goods, so their utility from generating waste corresponds to their utility from consuming goods. Meanwhile, as they dispose of waste, there will be a cost incurred to society as a whole, which is, the cost of waste disposal. Therefore, the social surplus from generating waste is equal to the utility of households from generating waste minus the cost of waste disposal.

The question that we now address is the socially optimal amount of waste, that is, the amount of waste that maximizes the social surplus. It can be shown that at the optimal amount, the marginal utility of households from generating waste must be equal to the marginal cost of waste disposal.

To see this reason, we first consider the amount of waste of X_1 in Fig. 5.1 as an example, where the marginal utility from generating waste (FX_1) is larger by FG than the marginal cost of waste disposal (GX_1). At this level of waste, if an additional unit is generated, the resulting incremental utility (FX_1) exceeds the resulting incremental cost (GX_1) by FG. Hence, X_1 is not an optimal amount of waste, as generating an additional unit of waste would result in an increase in social surplus (by FG). This case corresponds to consumption being curtailed excessively to reduce the amount of waste.

We next consider the amount of waste of X_2, where the marginal utility from generating waste (IX_2) is smaller by HI than the marginal cost of waste disposal (HX_2). This level of waste is not socially optimal, either; if waste is reduced by one unit, the utility from generating waste declines by IX_2, but at the same time, the disposal cost declines by a greater amount, HX_2, resulting in an increase in social surplus by HI. In general, as long as the marginal utility from generating waste is larger (smaller) than the marginal cost of waste disposal, the social surplus could be improved by increasing (decreasing) waste generation.

The social surplus is maximized when the amount of waste is X^*, where the marginal utility from generating waste is equal to the marginal cost of disposal. The social surplus is expressed in the figure as:

$$\text{(Social surplus)} = \text{area } AOX^*C - \text{area } OBCX^* = \text{area } ABC \tag{5.1}$$

where area AOX^*C expresses the utility of the households and area $OBCX^*$ corresponds to the disposal cost.

5.1.3 No Charges on Waste Disposal

Understanding the optimal amount of waste, we now examine how social surplus varies across the three policy options. We first consider a case in which there is no waste disposal fee ($P = 0$) and the disposal cost is covered by taxes such as resident taxes. When $P = 0$, the households generate waste in the amount of X_0. The benefit of the households, which is the utility from generating waste minus payment of the disposal fee, is represented by area $AOX_0 - 0 =$ area AOX_0.

We assume that the disposal cost is financed by revenue from resident taxes. Then, taxes from the residents are equal to the disposal cost, represented as area $OBEX_0$. The balance of the municipality's revenue and expenditure on waste management is the tax revenue minus the disposal cost, which is area $OBEX_0$ – area $OBEX_0 = 0$. The social surplus from generating waste is the benefit of the households minus the resident taxes plus the balance of surplus payments in the municipality. The balance of surplus payments is considered part of the social surplus because all surpluses will ultimately benefit the residents by being used to finance public services or as a source of tax relief in the municipality. By assumption, the municipality has a zero surplus and therefore we obtain:

$$\begin{aligned}\text{(Social surplus)} &= \text{(Household benefits)} - \text{(Resident tax burden)} \\ &\quad + \text{(Municipal surplus)} \\ &= \text{area ABC} - \text{area CEX}_0 \end{aligned} \tag{5.2}$$

By comparing Eqs. (5.1) and (5.2), we can see that the social surplus is smaller by area CEX_0 when the fee is not charged than when the optimal amount of waste is generated. This occurs because when disposal is free of charge, the amount of waste X_0 exceeds the optimal level X^*, where the marginal cost of disposal exceeds the marginal utility from waste generation.

5.1.4 A Flat Fee Pricing Scheme

Now let us consider the social surplus in the case of a flat fee pricing scheme where the municipality charges residents a fixed fee for disposal services (e.g., charging $100 annually on each household) to cover the entire cost of the services. Since the fee is the same regardless of the amount of waste generated, the fee burden will not vary across households, so there is no incentive for them to reduce waste. Therefore, the amount of waste generated is X_0, which is the same as in the case of no waste disposal fee. In this case, the disposal cost is area $OBEX_0$, so the municipality sets a fixed fee equal to area $OBEX_0$. Then, the households' benefit that includes the fee is the utility from waste generation minus the fee payment, which is expressed as area ABC minus area CEX_0. The municipality's balance of payments is zero, as the fee income equals the disposal cost. Again, we can calculate the social surplus by adding the household benefit and the municipal balance surpluses and therefore:

$$\text{(Social surplus)} = \text{area ABC} - \text{area CEX}_0$$

We can see that this social surplus is the same as that obtained by Eq. (5.2); in other words, the social surplus is the same between when no fee is charged and when a flat fee is charged. In both cases, the amount of waste exceeds the optimal level (X^*), and the social surplus is smaller by area CEX_0.

5.1.5 A Unit Pricing Scheme

Finally, let's consider a unit pricing scheme, also known as a "pay-as-you-throw (PAYT) program." This type of instrument charges households a disposal fee in proportion to the amount of waste that they generate. A common approach currently adopted in many municipalities in Japan is that households purchase designated trash bags in advance sold by the municipalities and use the prepaid bags in each collection period.

In the figure, the social surplus is greatest when the amount of waste is X^* and thus, the optimal unit price is P^*. The total amount that the households pay for waste disposal is the fee × the amount of waste (i.e., $P^* \times X^*$ = area OP^*CX^*), so the household benefit (which is, once again, the household utility from generating waste minus the fee payment) is area AP^*C. The fee revenue of the municipality, which is equal to the payment by the households, is area OP^*CX^*, and the disposal cost is area $OBCX^*$. Therefore, the balance of surplus payments in the municipality concerning the disposal services is:

$$\text{(Balance of surplus)} = \text{(Fee revenue)} - \text{(Disposal cost)} = \text{area } BP^*C \quad (5.3)$$

and there is a surplus in the balance of payments. We can see that if the fee is set at a level equal to the marginal cost of waste disposal, the amount of waste can be controlled to an optimal level and the social surplus can be maximized (area AP^*C + area BP^*C = area ABC).

5.1.6 No Charge, a Flat Fee, or a Unit Pricing?

Let us compare and summarize the outcomes of implementing the three schemes (i.e., no charge, a flat fee, and unit pricing for disposal services) and discuss some policy implications for waste management practices. We first show that when there is no charge for waste disposal, there is no incentive for waste generators (or households) to reduce waste, resulting in excessive waste generation. Because the disposal cost is borne by the households in the form of resident taxes, their burden increases as they generate excess waste, and therefore, the social surplus decreases. A flat fee pricing scheme does not maximize the social surplus either; the burden on households is the same regardless of the amount of waste that they generate and thus, the households are not incentivized to reduce waste.

The social surplus can be maximized by implementing a unit pricing scheme in which the fee is set at the level where the marginal utility (i.e., the demand curve) of waste generation equals the marginal cost of waste disposal. If the fee is set that way, the municipality will receive the fee revenue that exceeds the disposal cost, resulting in a surplus in the balance of payments as shown in Eq. (5.3). Because the households bear costs larger than the actual cost of disposal, objections may arise. However, from the point of view of maximizing social surplus, a surplus in itself is not a problem since it will ultimately be given back to the households in the form of funding for public services and tax breaks.

If the municipality lowers the fee to eliminate its surplus and to cover the cost exactly, the social surplus will not be maximized. Because waste disposal becomes more than the optimal level. Instead of lowering the fee, the municipality should refund the surplus to the households by reducing resident taxes for example.

5.2 Optimal Intergenerational Use of Landfills and Optimal Fee Policy

In the previous section, we examined whether a unit-pricing scheme for waste disposal would be effective in reducing waste. In the analysis, we focused on the current generation (i.e., those who currently live) without taking into account the existence of future generations (i.e., those who will live after the current generation). This section will extend the analysis to include an intergenerational perspective. When considering not only the current generation but also future generations, we should take into account the fact that landfills may not be unlimited. For countries with small land areas (e.g., Japan), in particular, landfills themselves are "precious resources" because it is often difficult to increase them due to various constraints on the construction. Given the shortage of landfills, it is necessary to consider how the final landfills should be utilized by the current and future generations and what kind of policies and practices should be implemented to achieve the desired outcome.

Below, we first explain the model for analysis. For simplicity, we will assume that there are only two generations: the current and future generations. Furthermore, to focus on the issue of landfills, we will not address environmental pollution caused by waste disposal. The analysis will demonstrate that the current waste policy is likely to lead to an overabundance of waste produced by the current generation, resulting in a shortage of landfills available for the future generation. We will also consider the pricing scheme that would lead to the optimal use of final landfills by the current and future generations.

5.2.1 The Model Setup

The discharged waste is reduced in volume through intermediate treatment such as incineration, and then disposed of at final landfills. If a certain fraction of the discharged waste is dumped in the final landfills, then the maximum amount of waste that can be discharged by both generations is determined by the capacity of the final landfill sites. This amount is hereafter called the amount of waste dischargeable. In this model, it is assumed that the capacity will not increase over time; in other words, new final landfill sites will not be built in the future so that the same sites are and will be used by the current and future generations, respectively. It is further assumed that the sites will be used up by both generations. In this setting, the sum of the total volume of waste generated by the current and future generations is equal to the amount of waste dischargeable.

Figure 5.2 illustrates the utilization of the final landfills between the two generations where the amount of waste dischargeable is $\bar{X}$. In the figure, the two vertical axes represent the disposal fees per unit of waste, and the D_c (D_f) represents the demand curve for disposal services by the current (future) generation of households. As in the previous analysis, we express the demand for disposal services in terms of the amount of waste generated. D_c (D_f) takes O_c (O_f) as the origin and measures the current (future) generation's waste on the horizontal axis to the right (left). For example, when the disposal fee is P_0, the amount of waste generated by the current (future) generation is O_cX_0 (O_fX_1). The demand curves are depicted as downward sloping in that waste generation decreases as the disposal fee increases. This implies that as the fee increases, households will make more efforts to produce less waste. MC_0 represents the marginal cost of waste disposal, i.e., the incremental cost incurred when an additional unit of waste is collected, incinerated, and finally dumped into the final landfills. Assume for simplicity that the marginal cost is constant and that the marginal cost is the same across the generations.

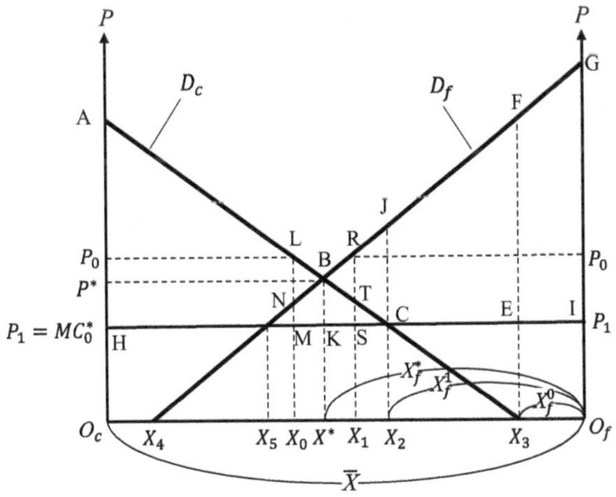

Fig. 5.2 Allocation of the final landfills between the two generations

5.2.2 Benefits for the Current and Future Generations When no Fee is Imposed

Using Fig. 5.2, we consider the amount of waste generated by each generation and the resultant social surpluses when no disposal fee is imposed on households. We first examine the current generation. Since the price of the disposal services is zero, households of the current generation produce waste in the amount of O_cX_3 and thereby obtain the utility expressed by area AO_cX_3. The benefit of the households from waste generation, which is the utility minus the fee payment, is also expressed by area AO_cX_3 due to the zero price of disposal services. On the other hand, the cost of disposal services to the municipality is expressed by area HO_cX_3E. We assume that the disposal services are just financed by the resident tax; in other words, the disposal cost (area HO_cX_3E) is equal to the resident tax paid by the households. Given that the households pay for the disposal cost through resident tax, the overall benefit of the households is obtained as the benefit from waste generation minus resident taxes, which is expressed as area AO_cX_3 – area HO_cX_3E or area AHC – area CX_3E. The municipality's surplus on waste management (i.e., resident taxes – the disposal costs) is zero by assumption. Therefore, the social surplus, defined as the sum of the overall household benefit and the municipality's surplus, is expressed as

$$\begin{aligned}\text{(Social surplus of the current generation)} &= \text{area AHC}-\text{area } CX_3E + 0\\ &= \text{area AHC}-\text{area } CX_3E\end{aligned}$$

Now let us turn to the future generation. Given the price of the services being zero, households of the future generation want to generate waste in the amount of O_fX_4. However, because the amount of waste dischargeable is constrained to be $\bar{X}$ and also because the amount disposed of by the current generation is O_cX_3, the future generation will only be able to generate waste in the amount of O_fX_3. The future generation's utility from generating the waste is represented as O_fX_3FG, which also exhibits the benefit of the households in the future generation from waste generation due to the zero price of disposal services. The municipal cost of the services is expressed as area O_fX_3EI, which is assumed to be equal to the amount of the resident tax burden. Therefore, the overall benefit of the households in the future generation (i.e., the benefit from waste disposal minus resident taxes) is expressed as area GFEI (area O_fX_3FG minus area O_fX_3EI). The municipality's surplus (i.e., resident taxes minus the disposal costs) is zero by assumption. It then follows that the social surplus of the future generation is obtained as:

$$\text{(Social surplus of the future generation)} = \text{area GFEI} + 0 = \text{area GFEI}$$

After examining both generations, we can now derive the total social surpluses of all generations by combining the social surplus of the current generation with that of the future generation. For simplicity, we assume that the discount rate[1] is zero (in other words, current benefits and future benefits are valued equally). Then, the total social surpluses of all generations are simply the sum of the social surplus of the two generations, which is expressed as follows:

$$\text{(Total social surpluses of the two generations)} = \text{area AHC} + \text{area GFEI} - \text{area } \mathrm{CX_3E} \tag{5.4}$$

5.2.3 *Marginal Social Surplus*

Here, we consider the incremental change in social surplus of the current (future) generation that would occur when the current (future) generation produces an additional unit of waste. This change will hereafter be referred to as "the marginal social surplus of the current (future) generation," thus playing an important role in the assessment of whether a particular combination of waste levels by the current and future generation is socially optimal.

As explained earlier, the social surplus is the sum of households' overall benefit (i.e., household utility minus resident taxes) and the municipality's surplus (i.e., resident tax revenues minus disposal cost). Assuming that the tax payment is equal to the tax revenue, the social surplus of the current generation is given as:

$$\text{(Social surplus of the current generation)} = \text{(Household utility of the current generation)} - \text{(Waste disposal cost of the current generation)} \tag{5.5}$$

An additional unit of waste generation influences not only the households' utility but also the disposal cost, ultimately changing the social surplus of the current generation. Therefore, Eq. (5.6), which is obtained from Eq. (5.5), implies that the change in the social surplus is equal to the change in utility minus the change in the disposal cost:

$$\text{(Change in the social surplus of the current generation)} = \text{(Change in the current generation's household utility)} - \text{(Change in the current generation's waste disposal cost)} \tag{5.6}$$

[1] The discount rate is the ratio of present value to future value. By using the discount rate, future value can be converted to present value. For example, if the discount rate is 10% per year, the value of US$ 1,100 received one year from now is equivalent to the value of US$ 1,000 today (= 1100 divided by (1 + 0.1)). If the discount rate is zero, the present value of US$ 1,000 is equivalent to the future value of US$ 1,000.

Given that we are considering an additional unit of waste generated, the left-hand side is "the marginal social surplus of the current generation,"[2] the first term of the right-hand side corresponds to the marginal utility (i.e., the incremental utility from generating an extra unit of waste), and the second term corresponds to the marginal cost of waste disposal (i.e., the incremental cost incurred when disposing of an extra unit of waste). Then Eq. (5.6) can be rewritten as

$$\text{(Marginal social surplus of the current generation)} = \text{(Marginal utility of the current generation's households)} \\ - \text{(Marginal cost of waste disposal of the current generation)}$$

Likewise, for the future generation, we obtain the following equation:

$$\text{(Marginal social surplus of the future generation)} = \text{(Marginal utility of the future generation's households)} \\ - \text{(Marginal cost of disposal of the future generation)}$$

5.2.4 *Do "No Disposal Fees" Maximize the Total Social Surplus of All Generations?*

Turning back to Fig. 5.2, we examine the marginal social surplus of the current and future generations when the current and future generations generate waste in the amount of O_cX_3 and O_fX_3, respectively. We will first consider the current generation. As is evident from the figure, the marginal utility is zero (recall that the demand curve represents the marginal utility curve), and the marginal cost of waste disposal is EX_3. Therefore, the marginal social surplus of the current generation is negative EX_3 ($= 0 - EX_3$). This means that an additional unit of waste generation will lower the social surplus by EX_3, because it does not change their utility (i.e., the marginal utility is zero), while increasing the disposal cost by EX_3. This result can also be interpreted as indicating that if the current generation reduces waste generation by one unit, the current generation's utility does not change, but the disposal cost decreases by EX_3, so that the social surplus of the current generation increases by EX_3.

We next examine the future generation. When the amount of waste generated by the future generation is O_fX_3, their marginal utility is FX_3, their marginal cost of disposal is EX_3, and therefore their marginal social surplus is FE ($= FX_3 - EX_3$). In other words, by increasing their waste generation by one unit, the disposal cost increases by EX_3, but their utility also increases by FX_3, so that their social surplus increases by FE. Combining these results, we can conclude that if O_cX_3 and O_fX_3 are the amount of waste generated by the current and future generations, respectively, the social surplus of the current and future generations would increase by EX_3 and FE, respectively, by reducing the current generation's waste by one

[2] It should be noted that upon one unit reduction in waste generation, the social surplus of the current generation decreases by the marginal social surplus.

unit and increasing the future generation's waste by that amount. These changes would lead to an increase in the total social surpluses of all generations by FX_3 while the total amount of waste generated by both generations remains the same. This result indicates that when a disposal fee is not charged, waste generated by the current generation will be excessive while waste by the future generation will be insufficient; the social surpluses of all generations cannot be maximized. To increase the total social surpluses of both generations, it is necessary to reduce the amount of waste by the current generation and increase the amount of waste by the future generation.

5.2.5 Conditions for Optimal Landfill Use Between the Generations

To what extent should the current generation reduce their waste and should the future generation increase their waste to maximize the total social surpluses? Let us first consider whether the total social surpluses of both generations are maximized when the current and future generations produce waste in the amount of O_cX_0 and O_fX_0, respectively. The marginal social surplus of the current generation is LM, which is the marginal utility (LX_0) minus the marginal disposal cost (MX_0). Likewise, for the future generation, the marginal social surplus is NM (= $NX_0 - MX_0$). Here, both marginal benefits are positive, and the marginal social surplus of the current generation exceeds that of the future generation (by LN). This condition implies that the total social surpluses of both generations are not maximized at this particular combination of waste levels (under the constraint that the amount of waste dischargeable is $\bar{X}$).

To see this, recall that (positive) marginal social surplus indicates an incremental increase in the benefit of the generation from increasing their waste by one unit; it can also be interpreted as indicating an incremental decrease in the social surplus of the generation from decreasing their waste by one unit. Thus, when the marginal benefit of the current generation is larger than that of the future generation, the total social surpluses of both generations can be increased, while the total amount of waste generated by both generations remains the same. Specifically, if the current generation increases their waste by one unit and at the same time the future generation reduces their waste by that amount, the total social surpluses of both generations will be increased (with no change in the total disposal) because the increase in the social surplus of the current generation (LM) outweighs the decrease in social surplus of the future generation (−NM).

What if the marginal social surplus of the future generation exceeds that of the current generation? As an example, we examine the case where the current and future generations produce O_cX_1 and O_fX_1, respectively; here, the marginal social surplus of the current generation, TS (= $TX_1 - SX_1$) is smaller than that of the future generation, RS (= $RX_1 - SX_1$). If the current generation reduces waste by one unit and at the same time the future generation increases waste by that amount, the total social surpluses of all generations will be increased without a change in the total amount of waste generated by both generations. This would occur because the decrease in the social surplus of the current generation (−TS) is smaller in magnitude than the increase in the social surplus of the future generation (RS).

Overall, these analyses demonstrate that if the marginal social surplus of the current generation exceeds the marginal social surplus of the future generation, the total social surpluses of all generations would be increased by increasing the current generation's waste and decreasing the future generation's waste by that amount. In contrast, if the marginal social surplus of the future generation exceeds the marginal social surplus of the current generation, the total social surplus of all generations would be increased by reducing the current generation's waste and increasing the future generation's waste by that amount.

The total social surplus is greatest when the waste produced by the current and future generations are O_cX^* and O_fX^*, respectively, where the marginal social surplus of the current generation is equal to the marginal social surplus of the future generation. In general, the condition for maximizing the total social surpluses of both generations is that the wastes generated by the current and future generations are set at a level where the marginal social surplus of the current generation is equal to the marginal social surplus of the future generation. At these levels of waste, we obtain:

$$\begin{aligned}&(\text{Social surplus of the current generation (i.e., its utility} - \text{its disposal cost)}) =\\&\quad \text{area } O_cABX^* - \text{area } O_cHKX^* = \text{area AHKB}\end{aligned}$$

and

$$\begin{aligned}&(\text{Social surplus of the future generation (i.e., its utility} - \text{its disposal cost)})\\&\quad = \text{area } O_fGBX^* - \text{area } O_fIKX^* = \text{area GIKB}\end{aligned}$$

It then follows that:

$$\begin{aligned}&(\text{Total social surpluses (i.e., social surplus of the current generation + social surplus of the future}\\&\quad \text{generation)}) = \text{area AHKB} + \text{area GIKB}\end{aligned} \tag{5.7}$$

By comparing Eqs. (5.4) to (5.7), we can see that the total social surpluses of all generations decrease by area BX_3F when there is no disposal fee. The no-disposal-fee policy leads the current generation to produce an excessive amount of waste, thereby having the future generation produce an insufficient amount of waste.

5.2.6 *Optimal Fees and Optimal Allocation of Waste Generation*

As discussed in Section I, even if a fee is imposed, a flat fee pricing scheme would not maximize the social surplus; rather, a disposal fee per unit of waste would be necessary to keep the waste produced by the current generation at an optimal level. How should the municipality set the fee per unit?

As explained earlier, the condition for maximizing the social surplus is that at the amount of waste produced by the current and future generations, their marginal social surpluses equalize. In Fig. 5.2, we can see that the marginal social surpluses of the two generations equal at point B where their demand curves for disposal services intersect. Therefore, by setting the disposal fee at P*, the amount of their waste can be directed to a level that maximizes the total social surpluses of two generations; it is O_cX^* for the current generation and thus, the future generation will be able to generate waste in the amount of O_fX^*, which is the same as the amount of waste that they want to generate at the disposal fee of P*.

Now let us compare the results when the future generation is not taken into account (as in Section I) and when it is (as in the discussion above). In Section I, we found that the social surplus is maximized by setting the level of the fee per unit equal to the marginal cost of disposal. When the future generation is taken into account, the optimal disposal fee is P*, which exceeds the marginal cost of disposal (P_1).

To what extent does the total social surpluses decrease if we set the fee equal to the marginal cost (i.e., P_1)? At this fee level, the current generation produces O_cX_2 while the future generation wants to produce O_fX_5. However, given that the amount of waste dischargeable is $\bar{X}$, the capacity left for the future generation is O_fX_2, which is smaller than O_fX_5. In other words, setting the fee at P_1 would result in having the current generation produce excessive waste and the future generation produce insufficient waste.

In this case, the household utility is area O_cACX_2 for the current generation and area O_fGJX_2 for the future generation, and the disposal fee is area O_cHCX_2 for the current generation and area O_fICX_2 for the future generation. Then the social surplus of the current generation is:

$$\text{(The utility of the current generation)} - \text{(The disposal cost)} = \text{area AHC}$$

Likewise, the social surplus of the future generation is:

$$\text{(The utility of the future generation)} - \text{(The disposal cost)} = \text{area GJCI}$$

Hence, the total social surpluses are:

$$\text{(Social surplus for the current generation)} + \text{(Social surplus for the future generation)}$$
$$= \text{area AHC} + \text{area GJCI}$$

As we can see from Eq. (5.5), setting the fee at P_1 results in smaller total social surpluses by area BCJ than setting it at P*.

5.2.7 *Existence of the Future Generation and Optimal Waste Management Policies*

Let us summarize some important points for the optimal waste management policy that takes into account the existence of the future generation. First, the optimal waste disposal fee that maximizes the total social surpluses of all generations must reflect not only the marginal cost of waste disposal but also the utility of the future generation (i.e., the marginal surplus of the future generations). Therefore, the fee should be charged in such a way that it is higher than the marginal disposal cost.

Second, given that the optimal waste disposal fee is higher than the marginal disposal cost, the revenue of the municipality from the fee exceeds the disposal cost and accordingly, the municipality in each generation will have a surplus in the balance of payments. Therefore, it is inappropriate for the municipality to reduce the disposal fee so that the surplus is zero, which means that the revenue from the disposal fee is equal to the total cost of waste treatment. The reason is that a disposal fee below the optimal level would result in an excess amount of waste by the current generation and an insufficient amount of waste by the future generation, which is not desirable from an intergenerational perspective.

Third and related to the previous point, if the waste disposal service becomes profitable by setting an optimal waste disposal fee, the surplus can be refunded to the residents. In such an instance, lowering the disposal fee may be the worse choice, as the undesirable consequences would occur as mentioned above. Other tax measures such as a reduction in the resident tax rate would be preferable.

Lastly, the social surplus would become smaller (larger) for the current (future) generation when the waste disposal fee is above the marginal disposal cost than when equal to the marginal cost. Upon raising the fee above the marginal disposal cost, the increase in the social surplus of the future generation outweighs the decrease in the social surplus of the current generation, and accordingly, the total social surpluses of both generations would increase. Therefore, the social surplus of the future generation should be increased at the expense of that of the current generation.

5.2.8 *Potential of Market Approaches to Optimizing Intergenerational Allocation of Landfills*

So far, we understand that the waste disposal fee must be set in such a way that the marginal social surplus of the current and future generations are equal; the fee level must correspond to the intersection of the current and future generations' demand curves as shown in Fig. 5.2. To set a fee this way, municipalities need to know the current and future generations' demand curves. However, it may be practically difficult, if not impossible, to accurately estimate the current generation's demand curve and/or the future generation's demand curve.

An alternative to optimizing waste disposal and maximizing total social surpluses across generations is market-based approaches where waste services are provided completely by private sectors instead of local government. In this approach, households and commercial establishments that generate solid waste sign contracts with private waste operators and pay them in exchange for the services. This approach has several advantages. First, the introduction of competition in waste management is expected to lower the disposal cost. Second and more importantly from an intergenerational perspective, it is expected that private waste operators provide the services by taking into account the demands of both the current and future generations. For example, if private waste operators predict the future demand for the services will be so large that they will be able to charge a higher fee for both generations, the operators will reduce waste services for the current generation and thereby leave more landfill capacity for future waste disposal. They would do so because that would be more profitable both at present and in the future.

More generally, as long as private waste operators pursue profit maximization, they will provide more waste services for the generation whose demand is relatively large, or equivalently, whose willingness to pay is relatively high to increase the sum of their profits from both current and future generations. As a result, private waste operators would unwittingly play a role in maximizing the total social surpluses of all generations. These arguments suggest that the introduction of a market mechanism into waste management will likely bring about desirable outcomes from an intergenerational perspective.

Third, unlike government organizations such as municipalities, private sectors can flexibly vary disposal fees. For example, fees will become high when the demand for waste disposal services increases due to an increase in waste, resulting from the booming economy. The fee increase would provide households/firms an incentive to reduce waste, preventing a decrease in the disposal capacity available for future generation. Changes in the fee level in response to demand may therefore help promote optimal use of landfills between the current and future generations.

Some might argue that we should not have private sectors provide waste services because it is difficult for them to accurately predict the demand of the future generation, and so their decisions can be wrong. Their wrong predictions may result in a misallocation of landfill capacity across generations. However, this possibility also applies to the case in which the local government provides the services; there is no guarantee that the government will be able to make better decisions than the private sector. Moreover, given that decision-making in government has often been influenced by political factors and pressure groups, desirable outcomes may be more likely obtained if all is left to the private sector.

It should be noted, however, that even if waste services are provided by private sectors, local government still needs to play key roles in waste management, such as curbing illegal dumping by increasing surveillance and penalties. The government should also implement measures to prevent environmental pollution at waste sites owned and managed by private sectors.

One may be skeptical about the market-based approach based on the idea that private sectors pursue their profit and consequently may disregard environmental protection. However, it is not necessarily the case that the environment will be adequately protected if waste is controlled by government or public sectors with no profit motive, as exemplified in the pollution problem at the landfill in Hinode-cho, Tokyo. Market forces may effectively prevent solid waste pollution and illegal dumping with the aid of measures that incentivize private sectors and waste generators to properly manage waste. The transfer of waste management from the government to the private sector may not be straightforward, given that various issues are involved, including landfill capacity, environmental risks, and illegal dumping of wastes. Nonetheless, it is worthwhile to consider the potential of the market mechanism to address problems associated with waste generation and disposal.

Box 5.1 Current Waste Situation in Japan

Under the Waste Management and Public Cleansing Act, waste is classified into two types: industrial and municipal solid waste. Industrial waste refers to waste generated by business activities. Twenty types of waste sources are defined by the Act as industrial wastes: ash, sludge, waste oil, waste acid and alkali, waste plastics, rubber and metal, waste glass, slag, debris, and dust. Municipal solid waste (MSW) refers to refuse and night soil, and waste other than industrial waste as defined by the Act. Among these two, wastes that are explosive, toxic, infectious, or harmful to human health and the living environment are specified as specially controlled industrial waste or specially controlled MSW, and must be kept under strict control throughout the process of collection, transportation, and disposal.

Waste disposal responsibilities were also defined in the Act. The disposal of industrial waste is the responsibility of the generators. They dispose their waste either by themselves or by commissioning a third-party contractor authorized by the local government. The disposal of MSW is the responsibility of municipalities and they dispose their waste similarly as generators of industrial waste do.

Figure 5.3 shows the changes in the total waste discharge and per capita waste generation per day in Japan. As shown in the figure, the total waste discharge peaked in FY2000 (54.83 million tons) and began to decline afterwards, with the amount at the end of FY2020 reduced by 24% from the peak to 41.67 million tons. Among the total waste generated in the country, 8.33 million tons were recycled, 29.76 million tons were reduced through intermediate treatment, and 3.64 million tons were for final disposal. This decrease resulted in a lower final disposal, which increased the remaining life expectancy of landfills (i.e., the number of years of remaining capacity) from 12.8 years on average nationwide at the end of FY2000 to about 22.4 years at the end of FY2020.

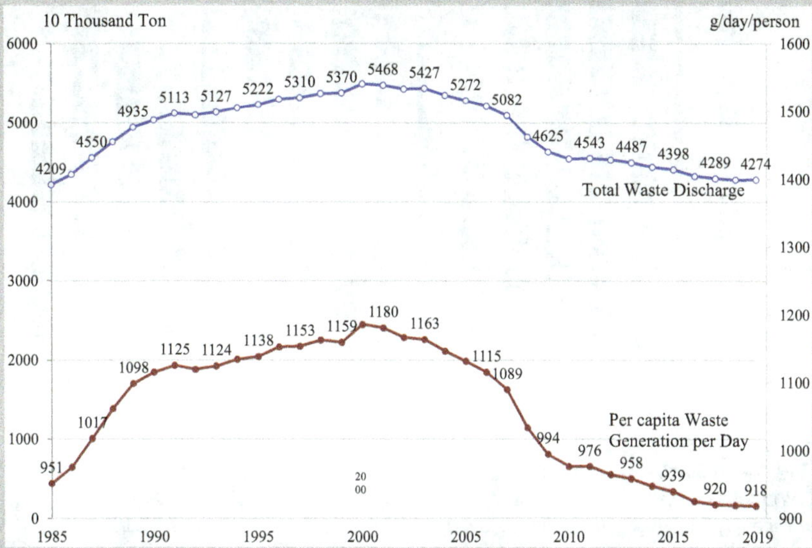

Fig. 5.3 Total waste discharge and per-capita waste generation per day in Japan. *Source* Ministry of the Environment (2022) "White Paper on Environment, Recycle Oriented Society and Biodiversity", https://www.env.go.jp/policy/hakusyo/r03/pdf/2_3.pdf (in Japanese) (last access date/ 2/23/2024)
Note 1: Based on the summary of FY2005 results, total waste discharge is "total MSW discharge," which is "amount of planned collection of MSW + amount of MSW directly brought in by individuals + amount of group collection of recyclable MSW" as defined in the Basic Policy for Comprehensive and Systematic Promotion of Measures on Waste Reduction and Other Proper Waste Management in the Waste Management and Public Cleansing Act
2: Per-capita waste generation per day was obtained by dividing the total waste discharge by the total population and by 365 or 366 days
3: The total population after FY2012 includes the foreign population

Figure 5.4 shows changes in the nation's industrial waste generation. The amount peaked in FY1996 (426 million tons) and declined to 385.96 million tons in FY2019, down by 9.4% from the peak. Of the total discharge, 203.57 million tons were recycled and 173.23 million tons were reduced through intermediate treatment, leaving 9.16 million tons for final disposal. Consequently, the remaining life of landfills for industrial waste increased from 3.1 years in FY1996 to 16.8 years at the end of FY2019.

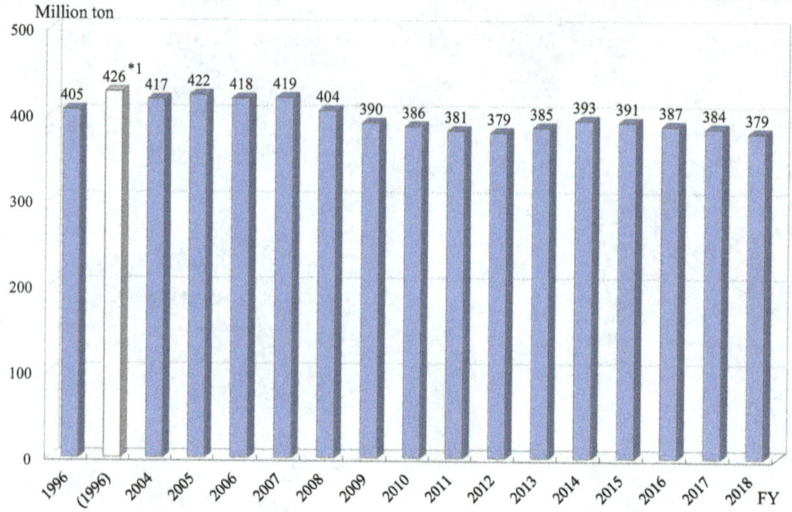

Fig. 5.4 Industrial waste discharge in Japan. *Source*: Ministry of the Environment (2022) "White Paper on Environment, Recycle Oriented Society and Biodiversity", https://www.env.go.jp/policy/hakusyo/r03/pdf/2_3.pdf (in Japanese) (last access date/ 2/23/2024)
*1: The amount of discharge shown above is the amount in FY1996 according to the "target amount of waste reduction" set by the government to be achieved by FY2010 (determined by the government on September 28, 1999) under the Basic Policy for Measures against Dioxin (determined by the Ministerial Meeting on Measures Against Dioxin)
Note 1: The method for calculating discharge amount has been partially changed since FY1996
2: The amount of discharge in FY1997 and thereafter is calculated under the same conditions as *1

Increased recycling contributed to the decrease in total waste generation. The amount of waste discharge has been continuously decreasing over the past 20 to 30 years owing to the introduction of recycling acts, disposal fees, and various other instruments. However, we must promote their sustainable use by establishing a sound material-cycle society as resources are finite. Enhancing recycling and waste reduction efforts will remain as important policy objectives.

Chapter 6
Precaution Against Environmental Accidents and Liability Rules for Damages

Akira Hibiki

Abstract Economic activities sometimes cause accidents that lead to environmental pollution and serious harm to society. Firms should take precautions against accidents. In this chapter, we explain how liability rules for damages give firms incentives to adopt precautionary measures. We also discuss how the socially optimal level of measures against accidents should be set and what is the optimal liability rule.

Keywords Precaution · Environmental accidents · Liability rules · Strict liability rule · Negligence rule · Judgement proof

The stranding of the Exxon Valdez in Alaska in March 1989 resulted in the largest oil spill in U.S. history, and the losses caused by the accident were extensive; it polluted about 2,000 km of coastline, killed hundreds and thousands of wild animals including seabirds, sea otters, and seals, and contaminated marine products, severely affecting the regional economy. According to Wan and Chen (2018), at least 80% of oil-tanker accidents involve human errors due to, for example, fatigue from overworking and lack of expertise.

Human factors also cause environmental accidents other than oil spills. The accident at Fukushima Daiichi nuclear power plant owned by the Tokyo Electronic Power Company (TEPCO) and subsequent radioactive contamination in 2011 were triggered by the tsunami after the Great East Japan Earthquake. The tsunami hit the plant and damaged its equipment, resulting in the loss of power at the plant which caused the contamination. It should be noted, however, that even before the earthquake, a large-scale earthquake had been predicted to hit the country, possibly causing a nuclear accident.

Proper countermeasures had been called for. Nevertheless, they had not been implemented where necessary. For example, emergency power supply facilities and fuel tanks were installed in coastal areas 4 m above sea level while countermeasures against a tsunami of up to 6.1 m had been assumed to be necessary. It is pointed out that a major factor of the nuclear accident is the failure to take sufficient precautionary measures. The effects of radioactive contamination from the accident are still present, incurring enormous damages.

T. H. Arimura and A. Hibiki, *Introduction to Environmental Economics and Policy in Japan*, https://doi.org/10.1007/978-981-97-2187-0_6

As the TEPCO's accident demonstrates, economic activities sometimes cause accidents that lead to environmental pollution and serious harm to society. Firms should take precautions against accidents. At the same time, institutional designs are necessary to give them incentives to adopt precautionary measures, given that the adoption incurs a significant financial burden to firms.

Liability rules for damages, which establish the liability of the injurer who caused an accident, give firms incentives for precaution against accidents. What liability rules for damages are socially desirable? To answer this question, in this chapter, we consider: (1) How should the socially optimal level of measures against accidents be set? and (2) What institutional designs are desirable to achieve that level of measure?

6.1 Optimal Precaution and Optimal Liability Rules for Damages[1]

6.1.1 *Social Costs and Optimal Precautionary Measures*

Avoiding accidents incurs various costs. For example, accidents due to machine malfunction can be prevented by the installation of safety devices that notify the operator when an abnormality occurs, but this countermeasure requires installation costs. The more precaution is taken to reduce accident probability and the harm caused by the accident, the greater the costs for implementing countermeasures.

What if firms are mandated to reduce the probability of an accident occurring to zero, and to take measures to reduce the damages to zero even when an accident occurs? The regulation would result in huge costs, making it difficult for firms to continue their production activities. Given that the production of goods has positive aspects that benefit society, it is not socially desirable to reduce harms caused by accidents to zero.[2]

The social costs of an accident are the sum of the amount of damages and the cost of measures against accidents. Because accidents are stochastic phenomena, the expected value of damages is used as an index for the damages caused by an accident. Even when damages caused by two accidents are the same amount, the accident damage that occurs with a 10% probability and the accident damage with a

[1] For a more detailed discussion, see Shavell (2004).

[2] For example, an advantage of reducing nuclear power generation all the way to zero is reducing the risk of radioactive contamination to zero. On the other hand, eliminating nuclear power generation may result in increasing the consumption of fossil fuels, and consequently may worsen the damage caused by global warming. Promoting renewable energy sources may increase the risk of power outage because the power supply is weather-dependent, making the supply unstable. Wind power may lead to increasing another environmental problem: health hazards from low-frequency noise. Implementing renewable energy will be significant financial burden to businesses and households (especially low-income households) through tax payment and higher electricity price. Evaluating the costs and benefits of reducing/adopting the respective energy sources is crucial for considering effective policy options.

Table 6.1 Firm's precautionary measures and social costs

Levels of measures	Cost of the measures	Accident probability (%)	Accident damages	Expected damages	Social costs
None	0	25	$10 million	$2.5 million	$2.5 million
Medium	$220,000	20		$2 million	$2.22 million
High	$1.25 million	10		$1 million	$2.25 million

1% chance of occurring are not the same because the latter is smaller than the former. That is: (the expected value of damages caused by an accident) = (the probability of the accident) × (damages caused by the accident). Using this equation, let us consider the following example to examine the level of measures that minimizes social costs, i.e., the socially optimal level of measures.

Table 6.1 shows the cost of measures, accident probability, and expected damages caused by an accident and its social costs, and they are shown in accordance with three levels of measures that the firm can take: none, medium, and high. Here we examine the case in which the probability of an accident changes depending on the level of measures taken by the firm. We assume for simplicity that damages caused by an accident are constant irrespective of the level of measures that the firm takes. For example, if the firm takes the "medium" level of measures, the cost of measures is $220,000 and expected damages are $2 million (10 million × 0.2), resulting in social costs of $2.22 million.

As shown in the table, the socially optimal level (i.e., the level that minimizes social costs) is the "medium" level of measures. Raising it to the "high" level will lower expected damages by $1 million while increasing the cost of measures by $1.03 million, resulting in an increase in social costs by $30,000. This means that it is socially not optimal for the firm to take the "high" level of measures; the additional cost of measures exceeds the expected damages that will be reduced, resulting in an increase in social costs.

6.1.2 *Firm's Precautionary Measures and Cost Under Liability Rules*

Three liability rules can be applied to firms: no liability rule, strict liability rule, and negligence rule. Under the rule of no liability, the firm is not liable for damages caused by the accident. Strict liability is a rule that requires the firm to compensate for damages when an accident occurs regardless of whether the firm is found to be at fault. Under the negligence rule, minimum standards for the measures that firms must take are established by law in advance. If an accident occurrs because a firm fails to meet the standards of measures, then the firm is found to be at fault and obligated

Table 6.2 Firm's precautionary measures and cost under the liability rules

Levels of measures	Firm's cost under no liability (=cost of measures)	Firm's cost under the strict liability rule (=social costs)	Firm's cost under the negligence rule
None	0	$2.5 million	$2.5 million
Medium	$220,000	$2.22 million	$220,000
High	$1.25 million	$2.25 million	$1.25 million

to compensate for damages. However, the firm is deemed to be nonnegligent and exempt from liability if it satisfies the standards.

Based on Table 6.1, we computed the firm's expected cost under these liability rules and presented in Table 6.2. The firm is not liable for damages under no liability, so it just bears the cost of measures as shown in the second column of Table 6.2. Given that the firm has an incentive to choose the level of measures whose cost is minimum, it chooses to adopt "none" of measures, which means that the socially optimal level of measures is not achieved. Under the strict liability rule, the firm's cost is the sum of the cost of measures and expected damages, which corresponds to social costs in Table 6.1. Strict liability gives the firm incentives to take the "medium," i.e., the socially optimal level of measures, as shown in the third column of Table 6.2. Here, choosing "none" is not desirable for the firm; by switching from "none" to "medium," the firm can reduce the total cost, as expected damages decrease by $500,000 even though the cost of measures increases by $220,000.

The firm's cost under the negligence rule is shown in the fourth column of Table 6.2. In making this computation, we assume that the legal standard of negligence is set at "medium," i.e., the level that minimizes social costs. If the firm chooses to take "none" of the measures, it will be found negligent and bear the cost of measures and expected damages. The firm will not be found negligent, however, if it chooses either the "medium" or "high" levels of measures. Then, the firm only bears the cost of measures. Given that the firm chooses what minimizes its cost burden, the firm takes the "medium" level ($220,000). The socially optimal level of measures is achieved also under the rule of negligence rule.

6.1.3 Which Liability Rule is Socially Desirable?

So far, we saw that the socially optimal level of measures is achieved both under the strict liability rule and the negligence rule. Recall, however, that the firm is liable for all damages under the strict liability rule whereas the negligence rule does not impose damages on the firm if it is found nonnegligent. In that case, the victim is not entitled to compensation for damages. Therefore, compared to the strict liability rule, the negligence rule tends to incur more cost to the victim and less cost to the firm. The strict liability rule may thus be considered more desirable than the negligence rule from a fairness perspective. The strict liability rule is superior to the negligence rule from perspectives other than fairness as well. Below we explain the advantages of the strict liability rule compared to the negligence rule.

(1) Under the negligence rule, the government needs to estimate the socially optimal level of measures that should be adopted by firms and set standards of negligence accordingly in advance. To do so, the government needs to know possible damages caused by an accident as well as accident probability when firms take precautions, which is not an easy task. In addition, the more accurate predictions they attempt to obtain, the more information they need, which incurs more costs. Such administrative costs do not incur under the strict liability rule, because the government does not need to make the computations.

(2) Damages caused by an accident usually vary depending on the circumstances. For example, suppose that a plant located in a highly populated area had an accident that caused environmental pollution. The accident and subsequent pollution would affect many people and cause substantial damage. However, damages would be smaller if the plant was located in a less densely populated area. If expected damages are large, stringent measures are desirable from the standpoint of minimizing social costs, whereas measures need not be so stringent if expected damages are relatively small.

Because the scale of damages differs depending on the circumstances, socially optimal measures vary as well. As such, standards of optimal measures must be established in accordance with different situations. This is practically not feasible as it would incur enormous costs. The optimal level of measures set under the negligence rule is not tailored to accommodate different circumstances, which means adopting the negligence rule results in large social costs. This sharply contrasts with the case of the strict liability rule under which the government does not need to establish standards of negligence in advance; the firm bears all social costs under the strict liability rule, so they choose the level of measures that minimizes their own cost (i.e., social costs) depending on the situation.

(3) Under the negligence rule, the court must judge if the firm is negligent (i.e., whether the firm satisfied the minimum standards of measures imposed by law), which incurs costs since evidence and investigation are necessary to make conclusions about the firm's negligence. These costs would not be incurred under the strict liability rule, as there is no need to judge the firm's negligence.

(4) Failure to gather sufficient evidence[3] may result in an erroneous judgement of the firm's negligence.[4] The firm is unlikely to be held liable for damages even

---

[3] Firms have accurate information about their actions, but they may withhold information from investigators if they know it will work against them. For this reason, there is an "information asymmetry" between the firms and investigators, or a difference in the amount of information available to the two parties.

[4] There are two types of erroneous determinations. The one is to determine that something nonnegligent as "negligent," and the other is to determine that something negligent as "not negligent."

Table 6.3 Erroneous judgement of negligence and changes in the firm's expected cost

Levels of measures	Cost of measures	Accident probability (%)	Accident damages	Social costs	Probability of erroneous judgement (%)	Firm's expected damages	Firm's total cost
None	0	25	$10 million	$2.5 million	95	$125,000	$125,000
Medium	$220,000	20		$2.22 million	95	0	$220,000
High	$1.25 million	10		$2.25 million	0	0	$1.25 million

when it is negligent if proving the negligence is difficult. In such a case the firm's expected cost becomes lower and he is not likely to take proper measures. Below we explain this point further with an example.

Based on Table 6.1, we show in Table 6.3 the case in which the court incorrectly determines the level of measures to be one level higher with a 95% chance (e.g., the firm adopted "none" of measures, but the court determined that it adopted the "medium" level of measures). The probability of an accident is 25% when the firm chooses "none." When an accident occurs, then the probability that the firm is held liable is 5%. Hence, the expected damages the firm bears are: $0.25 \times 0.05 \times 1000 =$ $125,000. The firm will choose to take "none" of the measures because the total cost (i.e., the sum of the cost of measures and expected damages) is lower than that of choosing the "medium" or "high" level of measures. This means the socially optimal level of measures will not be achieved.

6.2 The Judgment Proof Problem[5]

Damages caused by environmental pollution can be tremendous. If damages exceed the assets of the responsible firm, the firm is unable to pay fully the damages for which it is liable, and the maximum payment that the firm bears will be limited to the firm's assets. This is known as the "judgment-proof problem" (Shavell 1986). Below we consider how the firm's incentives for precaution are affected by being "judgment-proof," i.e., being unable to compensate for all of damages due to insufficient assets.

6.2.1 *Cases Where Firms Take Insufficient Precaution*

In Table 6.4, we calculate the firm's cost under the strict liability rule using the example in Table 6.1. Suppose that the firm's assets are $3 million, meaning that the maximum amount the firm can pay is its entire assets and it cannot pay fully the amount for which it has been found liable. Let us consider the firm's expected

[5] This section is written by simplifying formal analysis by Beard (1990)

payment for damages at the three levels of measures. By taking "none" of measures, the firm bears the expected payment of $750,000 (0.25 × 3 million = 750,000).

When the firm adopts the "medium" level of measures, the maximum amount of payment it bears is $2.78 million (i.e., the firm's assets minus the cost of measures, $220,000). So, the expected payment is $556,000 (0.2 × 2.78 million = 556,000), and the firm's total cost is $776,000 (556,000 + 22,000 = 776,000).

When the firm adopts the "high" level of measures, the firm's expected payment will be capped at $1.75 million, which is the balance of its assets after paying $1.25 million for adopting measures. So, the expected payment is $175,000 (0.1 × 1.75 million = 175,000) and the firm's total cost is $1.425 million (175,000 + 1.25 million = 1.425 million). Consequently, the firm will choose to take "none" of the measures and the socially optimal level of measures (which is "medium") will not be achieved. In this way, under the strict liability rule, the firm is not likely to take sufficient precautions when its assets are less than the damages it may cause.

Would we see the same outcome under the negligence rule? Table 6.5 presents the firm's cost under the negligence rule. When the firm takes "none" of precaution, it will be found at fault and its payment will be $3 million, the assets it owns. Hence, the firm's expected payment will be $750,000, and the amount will be the same as in the case under the strict liability rule. However, when the firm takes either the "medium" or "high" level of measures, it will be found nonnegligent and thus not be obliged to compensate for the damages; the only cost the firm bears is that of adopting measures. The firm will hence choose to take the "medium" level of measures, which means that the socially optimal level of precaution will be achieved.

As can be seen from the discussion above, the firm's incentives for precaution diverge under the two liability rules when the firm is judgment-proof; the socially optimal level of measures is not likely to be achieved under the strict liability rule, whereas the negligence rule is likely to give the firm incentives to take measures at

Table 6.4 Judgment proofing and the firm's cost under the strict liability rule

Levels of measures	Cost of measures	Accident probability (%)	Accident damages	Social costs	Firm's expected payment	Firm's total cost
None	0	25	$10 million	$2.5 million	$750,000	$750,000
Medium	$220,000	20		$2.22 million	$556,000	$776,000
High	$1.25 million	10		$2.25 million	$175,000	$1.425 million

Table 6.5 Judgement proofing and the firm's cost under the negligence rule

Levels of measures	Cost of measures	Accident probability (%)	Accident damages	Social costs	Firm's expected payment	Firm's total cost
None	0	25	$10 million	$2.5 million	$750,000	$750,000
Medium	$220,000	20		$2.22 million	0	$220,000
High	$1.25 million	10		$2.25 million	0	$1.25 million

Table 6.6 Judgment proofing and the firm's excessive precaution under the strict liability rule

Levels of measures	Cost of measures	Accident probability (%)	Accident damages	Social costs	Firm's expected payment	Firm's total cost
None	0	25	$10 million	$2.5 million	$2.375 million	$2.375 million
Medium	$220,000	20		$2.22 million	$1.856 million	$2.076 million
High	$1.25 million	10		$2.25 million	$825,000	$2.075 million

the socially optimal level.[6] For this reason, the adoption of the negligence rule is socially more desirable in situations where firms with insufficient assets may cause accidents that result in enormous damages.

6.2.2 *Cases Where Firms Take Excessive Precaution*

Let us turn to the case in which the strict liability rule gives the firm incentives for excessive precaution. Table 6.6 presents the firm's cost under the strict liability rule when the assets owned by the firm are $9.5 million. When the firm chooses to take "none" of precaution, the maximum amount of payment of the firm for damages is $9.5 million and its expected payment is $2.375 million ($0.25 \times 9.5$ million $=$ 2.375 million). When the firm takes the "medium" level of measures, the maximum amount of payment is $9.38 million (i.e., the assets minus $220,000 for implementing measures), and thus, the expected payment is $1.856 million ($0.2 \times 9.38$ million $=$ 1.856 million) and the firm's total cost is $2.076 million (1.856 million $+$ 220,000 $=$ 2.076 million).

When the firm takes the "high" level of measures, payment of the firm for the damages will be capped at $8.25 million, that is, the assets minus $1.25 million for adopting measures. The expected payment is therefore $825,000 ($0.1 \times 8.25$ million $=$ 825,000) and the total cost is $2.075 million (825,000 $+$ 1.25 million $=$ 2.075 million). Consequently, the firm will choose to take the "high" level of measures, which is higher than the socially optimal level, resulting in taking excessive precautions.

[6] When the assets owned by the firm are $880,000 and when the firm chooses to take "none" of precaution, the firm's expected payment are $220,000 ($880{,}000 \times 0.25 = 220{,}000$), which is the same amount as the firm's total cost of choosing the "medium" level of measures. This means that if the firm's assets are larger than $880,000, the firm will choose the "medium" level and the socially optimal level of measures will be achieved; the expected payment when the firm chooses "none" are greater than the total cost of taking the "medium" level of measures. However, if its assets are smaller than $880,000, the firm will choose to take "none" of precaution; the expected payments with this level of measures are smaller than the total cost of taking the "medium" level. Then, the socially optimal level of measures will not be achieved. In this way, when the firm's assets are very small, socially optimal measures are not implemented even under the negligence rule.

6.2.3 *Judgment Proofing and the Firm's Incentives for Precaution*

We observed above that when the firm's assets are less than the damages it may cause, the strict liability rule gives the firm incentives for excessive precaution at times and insufficient precaution at others. Below we explain why.

Let x be the cost of measures, and let accident probability be denoted by p(x), a function of x. Let us assume that the larger x is, the higher the safety and the lower the probability of an accident. That is, $p(x_0) > p(x_1)$ when $x_0 < x_1$. Suppose that the amount of damages is D and constant when the firm causes an accident. Then, when the cost of measures is x, social costs SC(x) are:

$$SC(x) = x + p(x)D$$

where the second term on the right-hand side of the equation represents the expected damages caused by the accident. The change in social costs when the cost of measures increases by one unit is:

$$SC(x + 1) - SC(x) = 1 - \{p(x) - p(x + 1)\}D \tag{6.1}$$

where the first number "1" on the right-hand side of the equation represents the increase in the cost of measures.

Since $p(x) - p(x + 1)$ (>0) denotes the decrease in accident probability due to the increase in the cost of measures, the second term on the right-hand side of the equation represents the decrease in expected damages due to the decrease in accident probability. Hence, the change in social costs (i.e., the left-hand side of the equation) equals the increase in the cost of measures (i.e., the first term on the right-hand side of the equation) minus the decrease in expected damages. If the increase in the cost of measures is smaller than the decrease in expected damages, the change in social costs will be negative, and social costs will decrease by increasing the cost of measures. Hence, it is socially desirable to increase the cost of measures.

When the firm owns assets W that are smaller than D, the firm's cost of choosing x under the strict liability rule, C(x), is:

$$C(x) = x + p(x)\{W - x\}.$$

Here, if the firm implements x, its assets will be W − x, so payment of the firm for the damages in the event of an accident is W − x. Therefore, the second term on the right-hand side of the equation denotes the expected payment of the firm for the damages when an accident occurs, which is smaller than expected damages p(x)D. The change in social costs as the firm increases the cost of measures by one unit is:

$$C(x + 1) - C(x) = 1 - \{p(x) - p(x + 1)\}\{W - x\} - p(x + 1) \tag{6.2}$$

The sum of the second and third terms on the right-hand side of Eq. (6.2) represents the reduction in expected payment due to the increased cost of measures. The second term represents the reduction in expected payment for the damages resulting from the decrease in accident probability. $p(x + 1)$ in the third term represents a decrease in the upper limit of the expected payment for damages[7] since an increase in the cost of measures reduces firm's assets by one unit (Let us call this the "subsidy effect").

Since $W < D$, it always follows that $\{p(x) - p(x + 1)\}\{W - x\} < \{p(x) - (x + 1)\}D$. If the subsidy effect is small, then:

$$\{p(x) - p(x + 1)\}\{W - x\} + p(x + 1) < \{p(x) - p(x + 1)\}D \qquad (6.3)$$

By comparing Eqs. (6.1) and (6.2), we obtain:

$$SC(x + 1) - SC(x) < C(x + 1) - C(x)$$

If $SC(x + 1) - SC(x) < 0 < C(x + 1) - C(x)$, then social costs will decrease by increasing the cost of measures. However, the firm will not do so because it is not willing to accept an increase in its cost burden. As a result, the cost of measures taken by the firm will be lower than the socially optimal level, which is what we observed in Table 6.4. Thus, the firm takes insufficient precaution.

Now, when $p(x + 1)$ is large, the inequality sign in Eq. (6.3) will be reversed:

$$\{p(x) - p(x + 1)\}\{W - x\} + p(x + 1) > \{p(x) - p(x + 1)\}D$$

By comparing Eqs. (6.1) and (6.2), we obtain:

$$SC(x + 1) - SC(x) > C(x + 1) - C(x)$$

If $SC(x + 1) - SC(x) > 0 > C(x + 1) - C(x)$, then social costs will increase due to an increase in the cost of measures; the firm will nonetheless increase the cost of measures because doing so will reduce the firm's total cost. As a result, the cost of measures will be higher than the socially optimal level, which is what we observed in Table 6.6. Thus, the firm takes excessive precautions.

The conclusions we reached can be summarized as follows. In circumstances where a firm is judgment-proof, it is socially more desirable to adopt the negligence rule than the strict liability rule. The socially optimal level of precaution is not achieved under the strict liability rule; the firm will take insufficient (excessive) measures when the subsidy effect of increasing the cost of measures is small (large). In contrast, the negligence rule leads the firm to take precautions at the socially optimal level even when the firm is judgment-proof but its assets are larger than a certain threshold. Given that the negligence rule does not give the firm incentives to take optimal measures when its assets are below the threshold, it may be desirable

[7] Since the amount of damages changes from $W - x$ to $W - (x + 1)$, the payment of the firm for damages decreases by one unit.

to introduce regulations on firms to allow only those with assets above a specific threshold to engage in production activities.

Box 6.1 Responding to the Risks Associated with Consuming Food and Using Products: Risk Information Disclosure and Consumer's Self-responsibilities

Various risks are associated with food and product consumption. For example, consuming food items containing soy or other allergenic ingredients without knowledge of the ingredients can be harmful to human health. Moreover, genetic modification contributes to higher-yield varieties and makes crops more resistant to diseases and pesticides, thereby increasing productivity and lowering food prices, but excessive consumption of genetically modified (GM) foods may also lead to health risks. Additionally, damages may occur owing to improper use or malfunction of products.

Air pollutants emitted by production or consumption activities harm other parties who are neither producers nor consumers of the products (i.e., third parties such as residents). Firms and consumers usually do not consider the health hazards or other adverse effects on third parties. Hence, policy instruments such as environmental taxes are necessary to control pollutant emissions and promote environmental conservation efforts. However, food consumers are affected by food risks. As the damage is not borne by a third party, no external costs are incurred. Therefore, imposing environmental taxes on contaminated food is not necessary.

If consumers are provided with accurate information on the health hazards involved (e.g., which food is contaminated, the probability and degree of contamination, and possible health risks of consuming the food), they will make the right decisions and avoid foods with a high risk of health hazards. People can choose which products to consume based on their risk level for certain allergies. For example, people will buy foods, if they are not allergic to any ingredients in those foods, while they will not buy them, if they are allergic to some ingredients. So if people are allergic to certain ingredients, producers can anticipate consumer behavior and stop producing high-risk foods. The consumer's decision does not affect the health of the other parties. Therefore, market failure does not occur, even in the absence of environmental taxes. It is essential for the government to provide consumers with accurate information about food safety; otherwise, consumers will not be able to make the right decisions.

However, it is not desirable to ban the overall production of high-risk foods to reduce risk to zero as it would lead producers to use higher-cost ingredients, resulting in higher production costs. Low-income households will be forced to buy higher-priced foods and, consequently, cannot afford other foods and fail to receive adequate nutrition. If GM foods are banned, the risks associated with their consumption will be eliminated, but it may lead to other health risks due to malnutrition. It is more beneficial for consumers to have access to more diverse product choices and to take responsibility for their own decisions.

It is essential for the government to provide consumers with accurate information about food safety; otherwise, consumers will not be able to make the right decisions.

However, it is not desirable to ban the overall production of high-risk foods to reduce risk to zero since it would lead producers to use higher-cost ingredients, resulting in higher production costs. Low-income households will be forced to buy higher-priced foods and, consequently, cannot afford other foods and fail to receive adequate nutrition. If GM foods are banned, the risks associated with their consumption will be eliminated, but it may lead to other health risks due to malnutrition. It is more beneficial for consumers to have access to more diverse product choices and to take responsibility for their own decisions.

It should be noted that, even if accurate information is provided, people with limited cognitive abilities to understand information, such as children and the elderly, may still make inappropriate decisions. This is particularly true when information is complicated or voluminous. They may consume high-risk products that they would not consume if they had sufficient abilities. Therefore, if such concerns are serious, the government should consider establishing food safety regulations and standards and providing easy-to-understand information through a system of labeling the presence or absence of certain ingredients and their level of risk.

References

Beard, R. (1990) "Bankruptcy and Care Choice", The Rand Journal of Economics, 21(4), 626–634.

Shavell, S. (1986) "The Judgment Proof Problem", International Review of Law and Economics, 6(1), 45–58. https://doi.org/10.1016/0144-8188(86)90038-4

Shavell, S. (2004) Foundations of Economic Analysis of Law, Harvard University Press, ISBN 9780674011557

Wan, Z. and Chen, J. (2018) "Human errors are behind most oil-tanker spills," Nature (2018-08-06), https://doi.org/10.1038/d41586-018-05852-0

Part II
Environmental Policy in Japan

Chapter 7
Recycling Laws and Their Evaluation in Japan

Akira Hibiki

Abstract In this chapter, firstly we explain the various recycling laws that have been enacted in recent years such as Container and Packaging Recycling Act, Home Appliance Recycling Act, Small Home Appliance Recycling Act, End-of-Life Vehicle Recycling Act, Construction Material Recycling Act, and Food Waste Recycling Act and discuss their problems. Second, we describe the "microplastics problem", a new emerging global waste problem, and its measures in Japan. Finely we discuss the policy against illegal dumping which occurs in the waste and recycling management.

Keywords Recycling laws · Microplastic pollution · Illegal dumping · Deposit-refund scheme

When we get utility from the consumption of goods and services, this consumption generates various types of waste. Food waste is generated, for example, when we cook and eat at home or have someone cook for us at restaurants. Either way, we are the generators—the only difference is whether we generate waste directly or indirectly. Likewise, when new houses or condominiums are built for sale, construction waste is generated. Many of us may not consider ourselves as generators unless we work in the construction sector. However, the root cause of industrial waste is our consumption, as housing is built to meet our household demand.

Consumption and production activities hinge on two precious resources: natural resources as raw materials essential for production and landfill sites where waste generated by consumption and production are to be disposed of. These resources are not unlimited. We will run out of natural resources if we use them faster than they can be regenerated. Landfills can also run out of space, and creating new sites is difficult due to land restrictions and the "not in my backyard" (NIMBY) syndrome among many other constraints. Optimal allocation of resources across generations is necessary for building a circular economy (See Chap. 4 for the analysis of optimizing the intergenerational allocation of landfills). Resource conservation for future generations, particularly, waste reduction and recycling are integral parts of waste management policy across regions and nations.

T. H. Arimura and A. Hibiki, *Introduction to Environmental Economics and Policy in Japan*, https://doi.org/10.1007/978-981-97-2187-0_7

This chapter reviews Japan's recycling policy programs. In what follows, individual recycling acts will be detailed, including the recycling guideline for disposable plastics that the government recently introduced in response to the growing concern about microplastic pollution. Policy measures to combat improper or illegal dumping will also be discussed, among which we will pay particular attention to deposit-refund schemes.

7.1 Recycling in Japan

Recycling in Japan has been conducted and promoted mainly in accordance with six individual recycling acts: (1) Container and Packaging Recycling Act, (2) Home Appliance Recycling Act, (3) Small Home Appliance Recycling Act, (4) End-of-Life Vehicle Recycling Act, (5) Construction Material Recycling Act, and (6) Food Waste Recycling Act.[1]

7.1.1 Container and Packaging Recycling Act

Containers and packaging wastes (e.g., paper, plastics, glass, and metals) account for more than half of household waste, taking up 66% of the volume and 28.5% of the weight of the entire household waste (The Ministry of the Environment (MOE), 2021).[2] To reduce the major waste source by requiring sorted collection and recycling of such items as glass bottles, cans, and PET bottles, the Container and Packaging Recycling Act was enacted in June 1995. The act partially took effect in 1997 and became fully enforced in 2000 by including more target materials, specifically, containers and packaging made of paper and plastic.

The act enabled the separation, recovery, and commercialization of many recyclables. Examples include aluminum (steel) cans collected and commercialized as aluminum raw materials (raw materials for ironmaking), glass bottles primarily recovered as raw materials for glass bottles and building materials, beverage cartons and cardboard containers recovered as papermaking raw materials. The list goes on; paper packaging recycled into various resources (such as papermaking materials, construction materials, and solid fuels), PET bottles recovered as plastic raw

---

[1] The full official names of these acts are 1) Act on the Promotion of Sorted Collection and Recycling of Containers and Packaging, 2) Law for the Recycling of Specified Kinds of Home Appliances, 3) Act on Promotion of Recycling of Small Waste Electrical and Electronic Equipment, 4) Law for the Recycling of End-of-Life Vehicles, 5) Law on Recycling of Construction-related Materials, and 6) Law for Promotion of Recycling and Related Activities for the Treatment of Cyclical Food Resources.

[2] MOE (2021), "Survey on use and disposal of containers and packaging waste." The survey has been conducted by the Ministry every year since 2006 and the results can be accessed online https://www.env.go.jp/recycle/yoki/c_2_research/index.html (in Japanese).

materials and polyester raw materials (such as fiber, sheets, and bottles), and plastic packaging reused as plastic raw materials, chemical raw materials, and fuels.

The recycling practices are promoted by the act requiring consumers to sort target containers/packaging upon disposal, the municipalities to collect them separately, and businesses that produce or use them for products (such as beverage manufacturers) to properly recycle them. Businesses can meet the requirement by recycling waste items either by themselves or by paying the recycling fee to the Japan Containers and Packaging Recycling Association (The JCPRA), a government-designated organization established under the act, and outsourcing the operation to the JCPRA.[3]

The JCPRA does not conduct recycling by itself but chooses recyclers every fiscal year through bidding. Recyclers sign an outsourcing contract with the JCPRA to be authorized to recover and commercialize collected wastes. Penalties apply to recyclers that do not fulfill or that underreport their recycling obligations. For example, a fine of up to JPY 1 million is imposed for failing to fulfill their obligation. Nonetheless, no penalties apply to consumers who do not follow the sorting guidelines, meaning that the act does not provide incentives for recycling to consumers. Put differently, it is up to individual consumers' consciences to determine whether they manually sort their waste daily.

The collection and recycling of beer bottles is distinctive in that the entire process is undertaken by the Beer Bottle Guarantee Deposit System, a voluntary initiative organized and managed by the Brewers Association of Japan. Under this system, a deposit of JPY 5 is paid by the retailer to the brewer/wholesaler for each bottle received. Consumers pay the same deposit to the retailer as part of the beer price and get refunded when they return the emptied bottles to the retailer.[4] The deposit refund increased the incentive to return bottles, with collection rates exceeding 95% after the system was introduced and reaching 99% by 2020.[5]

It should be noted that the system was launched partly because it is less expensive to reuse beer bottles than to manufacture new ones. As this case exemplifies, businesses engage in recycling voluntarily as part of market transactions if it is profitable for them to do so. However, the recycling of some products may result in additional costs, hindering voluntary initiatives among businesses. Government intervention will be needed in such situations to assist their recycling practices.

---

[3] They are obligated to recycle PET bottles, plastic containers and packaging, glass bottles, and paper containers and packaging, but not paper cartons, cardboard, aluminum and steel cans because they are considered of high value as resources and can be sold on the market for profit. More information on the system can be found at the JCPRA's website, https://www.jcpra.or.jp/english/tabid/603/index.php.

[4] This is a voluntary deposit-refund scheme and as such, some municipalities (or dealers) adopt the system while others do not.

[5] J4CE (2021) "Returnable beer bottle collection project", https://j4ce.env.go.jp/en/casestudy/101 (last access date/ 2/12/2024).

Table 7.1 Standards for recycling

	Sum of commercialization and heat recovery (%)	Commercialization (%)
Air conditioner	Above 80	Above 80
Television receiver with cathode ray tube	Above 75	Above 55
Television receiver with LCD/ plasma display	Above 74	Above 74
Refrigerator and freezer	Above 70	Above 70
Washer and dryer	Above 82	Above 82

Source MOE, http://www.env.go.jp/recycle/kaden/qa/q06.html#q34 (in Japanese) (last access date/ 2/12/2024)

7.1.2 Home Appliance Recycling Act[6]

Although waste home appliances contain useful resources such as iron, aluminum, and glass materials, they used to be dumped in landfills while only some metals like iron were recovered after shredding. These resources got recycled as the Home Appliance Recycling Act took effect in April 2001, targeting four types of home appliances: home air conditioners, TVs, refrigerators/freezers, and washers/dryers.

The act requires consumers to pay fees for the collection, transportation, and recycling of home appliances that they no longer want. Retailers are required to collect appliances from consumers and hand them over to manufacturers or importers, who must recycle them either by commercialization (i.e., recovering metal and glass materials contained in the appliances and reusing them as part of new products) or by heat recovery (i.e., using the heat generated by burning plastic wastes). When used appliances are shipped from consumers to retailers and then to manufacturers/ importers, the shipment is tracked by a manifest, or a document form required by the regulatory authority, to deter retailers from selling the appliances to second-hand dealers.

It is mandatory for manufacturers/importers to recover chlorofluorocarbons in air conditioners, refrigerators/freezers, washers, and heat-pump dryers. They are also obligated to recycle appliances in accordance with the standards set by the government. The standards specify the weight ratio of recovered parts or materials and the waste appliance, as shown in Table 7.1.

Recycling fees are set for each type of appliance based on size and manufacturer. Fees as of April 2022 are presented in Table 7.2. Collection and transportation fees vary by region and retailer. At major retailers and large appliance stores, consumers pay JPY 644–688 on average and JPY 1,050–1,500 at most to dispose of home appliances and replace them with new ones, and JPY 2,319–2,458 on average and

[6] Details of the act can be found at the MOE website, https://www.env.go.jp/content/900452888.pdf (last access date/ 2/12/2024).

Table 7.2 Recycling fees (April 2022)

	Recycling fees (tax included)
Air conditioner	JPY 990–2,000
Cathode ray tube TV (Smaller than 15 inches)	JPY 1,320–3,100
Cathode ray tube TV (Larger than 16 inches)	JPY 2,420–3,700
LCD and plasma TV (Smaller than 15 inches)	JPY 1,870–3,100
LCD and plasma TV (Larger than 16 inches)	JPY 2,970–3,700
Refrigerator and freezer (Smaller than 170L)	JPY 3,740–5,200
Refrigerator and freezer (Larger than 171L)	JPY 4,730–5,600
Washer and dryer	JPY 2,530–3,300

Source The Association for Electric Home Appliances of Japan, https://www.rkc.aeha.or.jp/cms/wp-content/uploads/recycle_price_list_2022-1.pdf, (in Japanese) created by the authors (last access date/ 2/12/2024)

JPY 4,200 at most for disposal only.[7] In the case of smaller appliance stores in the suburbs, they pay JPY 2,026–2,632 on average and JPY 29,215–42,000 at most for disposal and replacement, and JPY 2,451–3,086 on average and JPY 15,000–23,925 at most for disposal only. We can see that the fees tend to be smaller in urban regions where major retailers are more likely available compared to rural areas.

As the fees are not insignificant, some consumers illicitly dump their home appliances to avoid the burden. Local governments attempt to raise public awareness against illegal dumping by patrol monitoring, installing surveillance cameras, and placing posters and signboards. These countermeasures have been effective to some extent; the number of illegally dumped items decreased approximately by 68% from 2002 to 2020 (from 164,678 to 53,195 items).[8]

The number of illegally dumped home appliances can further be reduced if the current pay-after-use system is modified to incorporate a deposit-refund scheme. Assume that the consumer purchases a large refrigerator and pays a deposit of JPY 10,000 at the time of purchase. By returning the refrigerator to a retailer for disposal, the consumer can obtain a refund, which is JPY 10,000 minus the actual costs of collection, transportation, and recycling. At present, suburban smaller-scale retailers charge JPY 3,000 on average for collecting and transporting a large refrigerator in addition to JPY 5,600 at most as the recycling fee,[9] meaning that the consumer can

[7] Based on the survey on collection and transportation fees under Home Appliance Recycling Law. The survey result was reported in 2006 at the joint meeting of the Central Environmental Council in MOE and the Industrial Structure Council in the Ministry of Economy, Trade and Industry (METI). The full version of the survey is available online at https://www.env.go.jp/council/former2013/03haiki/y0311-13/ref04.pdf. (in Japaese) (last access date/ 2/12/2024).

[8] Among the 53,195 items, 1,207 was air conditioners, 31,827 televisions, 11,724 refrigerators/freezers, and 8,437 washers/dryers. Further details on illegally dumped home appliances are available at the MOE website, https://www.env.go.jp/recycle/kaden/fuho/index.html (in Japanese) (last access date/ 2/12/2024).

[9] The estimates are based on "Survey on collection and transportation fees under Home Appliance Recycling Law" reported at the joint meeting of the Councils in the MOE and METI.

obtain a refund of at least JPY 1,400 (or larger if the fees are lower). The incentive element encourages the consumer to choose proper disposal over illegal dumping. For cases where the total costs of disposal and recycling are higher than the deposit amount, consumers may be required to pay the deficit at the time of disposal. In such cases, we can prevent illegal dumping simply by elevating the deposit amount.

One may argue that deposit-refund schemes are not desirable as they increase the burden on consumers by having them pay higher prices for goods and services. Although the waste-end charge system as currently adopted makes products appear cheaper on store shelves, consumers still pay for the cost of disposal and recycling. It is a matter of *when* to pay the costs, that is, paying it either at the time of purchase (deposit-refund schemes) or at the time of disposal (pay-after-use-system). If the consumer receives a refund, which is the deposit with interest based on the period between the time of purchase and the time of disposal, the cost to the consumer will be the same as in the pay-after-use system.

A crucial difference is that a back-end charge system allows illegal dumpers to get away with not paying the disposal/recycling fees while a deposit-refund scheme selectively penalizes consumers who improperly discharge their waste as they fail to get their deposit refunded. Put differently, arguing against deposit-refund schemes leads to protecting the interests of (potential) illegal dumpers. Another advantage of a deposit-refund is in that, as this market instrument introduces an incentive to properly dispose of wastes, it will reduce or eliminate the associated expense of monitoring.

7.1.3 Small Home Appliance Recycling Act

Small home appliances and consumer electronics such as smartphones, digital cameras, and game machines make extensive use of rare earth metals and other rare elements, most of which used to be discarded as trash after only one use. Because the net social benefit of recovering these rare elements is significant, the government launched the Small Home Appliance Recycling Act on April 1st, 2013 to ensure that consumer electronics would be collected, sorted, and properly recycled. Unlike the Home Appliance Recycling Act whose policy programs are implemented uniformly across the nation, this act gives decision-making authority to local governments and officials. This means that they are to develop and implement their own plans by establishing recycling fees, recycling targets, and methods of collection, sorting, and recycling.

At present, recycling efforts at the municipal level largely depend on consumers' willingness and voluntary action. Some municipalities provide drop-off boxes in appliance stores and public facilities for consumers to stop by and return waste items. Because no refund is given for returning waste, the system does not introduce an incentive for proper disposal and recycling. Likewise, initiatives by manufacturers, retailers, and recyclers currently play key roles in the recovery, reuse, and remanufacture of small home appliances in municipalities where recycling services are provided free of charge. As in the case of home appliances, deposit-refund schemes seem to be a viable policy option to further enhance recycling rates and practices.

7.1.4 End-of-Life Vehicle Recycling Act

Conventionally, end-of-life vehicles used to be bought by dismantlers (shredders) to dismantle (shred) and recover reusable parts and materials including steel and non-steel metal scrap. While they were sold for remanufacturing, the rest known as automobile shredder residue (ASR), consisting of materials such as plastics, glasses, and rubber, ended up in landfills. The reduction and reuse of ASR were needed because many industrial waste landfills were expected to run out of space. Meanwhile, the abandonment and improper disposal of vehicles and auto parts was becoming a problem, which was caused partly by a higher disposal fee imposed on vehicle owners due to the elevated costs of treatment and recovery and the stagnating price of scrap metal. In response to the problems, the government enacted the End-of-Life Vehicle Recycling Act in 2002 (which came into full effect in January 2005) and promoted the recycling of ASR into resources (e.g., welding slag and useful gas) as well as the use of waste heat recovery system which captures the waste heat and transferred it as an energy source.

One of the main objectives of the act is to mandate manufacturers/importers to collect and properly treat ASR, airbags, and chlorofluorocarbons that are used in air conditioners. The act also directs that new car buyers must pay a deposit for recycling at the time of purchase to the Japan Automobile Recycling Promotion Center, the fund management corporation designated by the government, and receive recycling tickets in exchange. When returning unwanted vehicles for recycling, they hand the tickets to dismantling or shredding companies and then receive a refund. If they sell their vehicles in the second-hand market, the tickets can be transferred to the next owner. The deposit amount depends on the type of vehicle and manufacturer, as it is based on the cost of processing ASR, airbags, and chlorofluorocarbons. A standard passenger vehicle, for example, costs from JPY 6,000 to 18,000.[10]

According to the recycling statistics, the act successfully facilitated the recycling of end-of-life vehicles; recycling rates for ASR and airbags were 92–94% and 92–100%, respectively, in FY2011, meaning that nearly all ASR and airbags collected were recycled.[11] The number of abandoned or improperly stored vehicles sharply dropped across the nation following the launch of the act, from 218,000 in FY 2010 before the act was implemented to 8,667 at the end of FY 2011, which is a decrease by 96% (see Fig. 7.1). The results indicate that illegal dumping can be significantly

---

[10] Full details of the fees are available at the Japan Automobile Recycle System website, http://www.jars.gr.jp. (in Japanese) (last access date/ 2/12/2024).

[11] Details on automobile recycling rates and processes (albeit not recent) are available at the MOE website, https://www.env.go.jp/recycle/car/situation1.html.

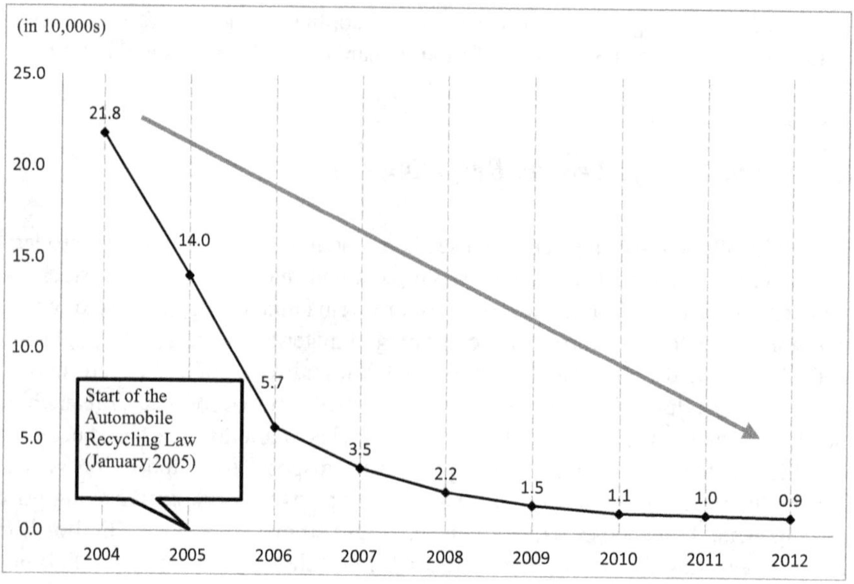

Fig. 7.1 Illegal dumping and improper storage of vehicles in Japan. *Sources* MOE "Recycling of the Automobile", https://www.env.go.jp/recycle/car/situation1.html (in Japanese) adopted by the authors (last access date/ 2/12/2024)

discouraged by a deposit-refund scheme that reduces the consumers' costs at the time of disposal.

7.1.5 Construction Material Recycling Act[12]

Before the Construction Material Recycling Act was enacted in May 2000, construction waste such as concrete and asphalt masses and wood waste used to account for a large proportion of waste: about 20% of industrial waste and the final disposal waste (i.e., waste that was landfilled after going through the intermediate treatment process for reduction and recycling) and about 60% of illegally disposed waste.[13] As a legal measure for reducing construction waste and preventing illegal dumping, the act directs that contractors engaged in construction projects above a certain size must separate, dismantle, and recycle their waste materials if they belong to the following categories: demolition of a building with a floor area greater than $80m^2$, new construction or expansion of a building with a floor area greater than $500m^2$, building repair ·

[12] The official name of the law is "the Law on Recycling of Construction-related Materials."

[13] MOE, https://www.env.go.jp/recycle/build/gaiyo.html (in Japanese) (last access date/ 2/12/2024).

and redecoration whose contract prices are larger than JPY 100 million, and demolition or new construction of structures other than buildings whose contract prices are larger than JPY 5 million.

The act also directs the recycling of various construction materials. Examples include concrete mass that is mainly reused as roadbed material, asphalt concrete mass reused as roadbeds and pavements, and construction-generated wood that is turned into wood chips for biofuels and construction boards. It is also the legal obligation of contractors to properly treat and dispose of chemicals and toxic substances used or generated in the construction process. Construction materials contain toxic and hazardous materials that, if improperly managed or abandoned, can result in hazardous waste contamination and pose a significant threat to health and the environment.

The Ministry of Land, Infrastructure, Transport and Tourism (MLIT)[14] reported that construction waste was reduced by 85% after instituting the act from 12.85 million tons in 2000 to 2.12 million tons in 2018. Successful outcomes are also observed in recycling rates, as they either exceeded or almost met the objectives of the 2014 Construction Recycling Promotion Plan. Specifically, recycling and reduction rates for construction waste and recycling rates for construction-generated soil were 97.2% and 79.8%, respectively, in 2018 whereas their target rates are 96% and 80%, respectively. Likewise, illegal dumping of construction waste was reduced by 87.5%, from 303,997.8 tons in 1999 to 38,110 tons in 2020. Therefore, it can be concluded that the Construction Material Recycling Act is effective in reducing the illegal dumping of construction waste. It should be noted that it accounts for a substantial portion of illegally dumped waste (71.4% in 1999 and 74% in 2020), suggesting the need for further measures against illegal dumping.

7.1.6 Food Waste Recycling Act

It is reported that 25.31 million tons of food was wasted in FY 2018 in Japan of which 7.66 million tons were generated from households, 17.65 million tons from businesses, and 6 million tons as food loss (i.e., food that is discarded although edible), which accounts for more than a quarter of the wasted food.[15] Businesses and households are two major sources of food loss; half of the food loss consists of edible food that was not purchased by consumers at retailers such as supermarkets and convenience stores, food items returned by consumers at retailers, as well as

[14] MLIT (2020) "FY 2018 Survey on Construction Byproducts (Finalized Values)," https://www.mlit.go.jp/report/press/content/001334705.pdf (in Japanese) (final access date: 2/12/2024).

[15] MOE, "Publication of Estimated Amounts of Food Waste and Food Losses in Japan (FY2008)" https://www.env.go.jp/press/109519.html (in Japanese) (last access date/ 2/12/2024).

leftovers at restaurants and substandard products, while the other half is generated at households as leftovers or food purchased but discarded without being used.[16]

The Food Waste Recycling Act was enacted in May 2001 as a policy initiative aimed at reducing food loss and waste generated by businesses and sectors of the food industry (e.g., food manufacturers and processors, wholesalers, retailers, and restaurants). The act establishes recycling targets called "the target percentage" and "the standard target percentage" for each sector and individual businesses.

The target percentage is calculated as:

$$\frac{\text{Waste reduction rate} + \text{Amount recycled} + \text{Reduction in weight} + 0.95 \times \text{ Heat recovery}}{\text{Potential waste generation } (= \text{ Actual waste generation rate} + \text{Waste reduction rate}).}$$

The target percentage[17] for FY2024 is 95% for food manufacturers, 75% for food wholesalers, 60% for food retailers, and 50% for food service providers. All sectors increased their recycling rates over the period from FY2008 to FY2021[18]: food manufacturers increased from 93 to 96%, food wholesalers from 59 to 70%, food retailers from 37 to 55%, and food service providers from 13 to 35%. We can see that the food retailers and food service providers particularly made a significant improvement. Recycling rates for the entire food industry altogether increased from 79 to 87%.

The act directs that businesses that generate over 100 tons of food waste annually will be given recommendations, public announcements, orders, and/or fines and those that generate less per year be given guidance and advice if their reduction and recycling efforts are insufficient. This scheme faces challenges, however, as it is difficult to estimate the amount of food waste generated by each business every year, particularly given that many businesses are small-sized enterprises. Consequently, waste reduction efforts are largely driven by individual businesses at present. For example, major convenience stores and supermarket chains donate products nearing expiration dates to food banks. They also promote expiring products by giving bonus points to consumers who purchase them with e-money. In addition, they recycle expired products into livestock feed and fertilizers. While these initiatives are causing successful outcomes, also desirable are policy interventions aimed at altering behaviors and practices among consumers and smaller-sized businesses because they too are the dominant generators of food waste.

---

[16] The Ministry of Agriculture, Forestry and Fisheries. (2020, October). The State of Food Loss and Waste. *Aff*, https://www.maff.go.jp/j/pr/aff/2010/pdf/aff2010_all.pdf (in Japanese) (last access date/ 2/12/2024).

[17] The Ministry of Agriculture, Forestry and Fisheries (MAFF), "Targets for recycling of food waste", at https://www.maff.go.jp/j/shokusan/recycle/syokuhin/s_info/saiseiriyo_mokuhyou.html (in Japanese) (last access date/ 2/12/2024).

[18] MAFF "Annual amount of food waste and its recycling rate", https://www.maff.go.jp/j/shokusan/recycle/syokuhin/kouhyou.html (in Japanese) (last access date/ 2/12/2024).

7.2 Microplastic Pollution

Pollution caused by **microplastics**, or plastic debris less than 5 mm in diameter, is a global concern as expressed at the 2015 G7 summit in Germany. Chemicals contained in or absorbed by microplastics negatively impact ecosystems through the food chain, though the full extent of impacts remains under-researched. Microplastics are classified into two types: **primary microplastics** and **secondary microplastics**. Primary microplastics are micro-sized plastics such as microbeads used in a variety of products that we use every day. Products that use microbeads include toothpaste, shampoos and conditioners, sunscreen, face and body washes, bath salts, mouth-washes, lipsticks, eyeliners, and foundation. By using these items, we unconsciously cause environmental pollution because microbeads are discharged into the natural environment through sewage.

Being so small, microbeads are difficult to recover once released into the environment. The United States, France, South Korea, the United Kingdom, Taiwan, New Zealand, and Canada have banned the manufacture of products containing microbeads, and some of them also banned the distribution and importation of the products. Policy instruments of this kind are yet to be implemented in Japan while initiatives at the voluntary level were launched subsequently after the Japan Cosmetic Industry Federation asked its member companies to self-regulate and remove products that contain microplastics in March 2016.

Disposable plastic products such as water bottles, plastic straws, and containers turn to small particles called secondary microplastics due to gradual degradation caused by ultraviolet light and external forces like ocean waves. The majority of microplastics found in the oceans and ingested by marine animals are secondary microplastics. Incidents of microplastic ingestion are widely reported, including sea turtles and whales that ate plastic litter accidentally and plastics found in the stomachs of seabirds in the North Pacific and in the feces of fur seals in the Antarctic Ocean. While versatile and useful, disposable plastic products need to be recovered before degradation begins, as they persist for decades or hundreds of years and harm the environment and wildlife.

Jambeck et al. (2015) reported that the annual emission of plastic waste into the oceans is estimated to be between 4.8–12.7 million tons for which Asia is mostly responsible. The largest amount is generated in China (3.53 million tons/year), followed by Indonesia (1.29 million tons/year), Philippines (075 million tons/year), Vietnam (0.73 million tons/ycar), and Sri Lanka (0.64 million tons/year) with Japan (0.06 million tons/year) and the U.S. (0.11 million tons/year) ranked 20th and 30th, respectively. The quantity is expected to increase further, as countries in Asia will increase consumption in line with their high economic growth. Plastic waste reduction across Asian countries, including Japan, is thus essential in tackling microplastic pollution.

Plastic waste can be reduced by using substitute materials, specifically, **bioplastics** known as **biomass plastics** that are made from renewable organic resources and **biodegradable plastics** that are made from micro-organisms and that eventually decompose into water and carbon dioxide. Biomass plastics are made from such products as corn, sugarcane, cassava, oil palm, and soybeans. If they are used to produce biomass plastics, their demand would increase and then food prices could be affected. Merits and demerits are also pointed out about biodegradable plastics. While they can be made harmless by decomposition, they take quite a long time to decompose if they are discharged into the ocean and cause microplastic pollution just like conventional plastics.

The Act on Promotion of Resource Circulation for Plastics came into force in April 2022 to facilitate the circulation of plastics across the entire life cycle (i.e., from product design to waste disposal) by involving all entities that produce, distribute, and use plastic materials and products. The act targets 12 disposable products: spoons, forks, knives, stir sticks and straws for drinks, toothbrushes, hairbrushes, combs, razors, shower caps, clothes hangers, and garment covers. Businesses whose annual use of these products exceeds 5 tons must promote source reduction practices.[19] Accordingly, businesses started to develop and implement initiatives on their own.[20] For example, food-service operators like *Ohsho Food Service Corp.* began to charge customers for spoons to takeout, while others like the convenience store operator *FamilyMart Co.* eliminated the provision of plastic utensils. Replacing plastic items with alternatives is another commonly adopted strategy; the restaurant chain *Ringer Hut* uses spoons made up of 25% of plant-derived materials, and *Imperial Hotel, Ltd.* provides toothbrushes and other complimentary amenities made from bamboo or wood.

It should be noted that plastic products covered by the act account only for about 1% of Japan's plastic waste. For better recycling outcomes, it is necessary to broaden the scope of target products. Besides, implementing a deposit-refund scheme would be a sensible measure, as it works against littering and improper disposal by providing incentives for consumers to return plastic waste before degradation begins. Improved waste management systems, better product design, and control measures against the release of plastic waste into the oceans are needed as part of the policy initiatives for a more sustainable future.

7.3 Preventing Waste Scattering and Illegal Dumping

Earlier in the chapter, we discussed that some individuals and businesses choose to illegally dump their waste when recycling fees are required at the time of disposal, as in the case with unwanted home appliances and construction waste. The same happens with a waste disposal fee (see Chap. 5 for the economic analysis of

[19] The targeted industries are retailers and service providers, food and beverage retailers, non-store retailers, accommodations, restaurants, take-out and delivery food services, and laundry services.

[20] The Nikkei. (2022, April 1) "Disposable Plastics: Companies Obligated to Reduce from April, Switch to Alternative Materials", https://www.nikkei.com/article/DGXZQOUA300BS0Q2A330C2000000/.

disposal charges). Policy interventions are necessary to discourage and reduce illegal dumping, as it weakens the effectiveness of instruments for proper waste management and recycling. This section will consider countermeasures against illegal dumping, specifically, deposit-refunds and penal regulations. It will be argued that adopting a deposit-refund scheme to collect as many types of waste as possible is desirable to discourage roadside litter and illegal dumping. When it is not feasible to implement the system, penal regulations are desirable as a substitute measure.

7.3.1 Deposit-Refund Scheme

A deposit-refund scheme is an effective instrument to prevent illegal dumping, as it provides consumers with incentives to properly dispose of waste for recycling. Some regions in Japan have adopted the system for collecting cans. Consumers pay the initial deposit when purchasing canned beverages and then obtain a refund—either the full or a partial amount of the deposit—upon returning empty cans to collection machines or retailers. The system is aimed to promote responsible disposal and reduce roadside litter. Similar schemes abound overseas. Beverage containers of some or all kinds are collected under deposit-refund schemes in the U.S. and Europe. South Korea uses the system to collect not only beverage containers but also various wastes including televisions, washing machines, air conditioners, tires, lead-acid batteries, as well as containers of liquor, cosmetics, and lubricating oil.

The deposit-refund scheme is particularly suitable for collecting hazardous waste such as pesticides, lead-acid batteries, and gas cylinders that contain toxic, flammable, corrosive, or explosive substances. If these types of waste are placed in and mixed with ordinary solid waste, they can cause fires, explosions, and pollution, posing a threat to the environment and the health of animals and humans. The negative externalities can be alleviated by instituting a deposit-refund scheme and properly collecting hazardous waste.

Some problems may arise if the scheme is instituted in some regions but not in others. Suppose that consumers purchase goods in a region that does not adopt the scheme and then return them to collection points in regions that adopt the scheme. There will be no refund in this case. As such, the policy practice does not provide consumers with incentives for recycling and hence, not prevent littering or the mixing of contaminants or recyclables with non-recyclables.

One may propose to give refunds to consumers even if they have not paid deposits. While this may reduce roadside litter, illegal dumping, and associated environmental degradation, it will lead to some other problems. First, some consumers may take advantage of the loophole, buying products in regions not implementing the deposit-refund scheme and returning them in regions adopting the scheme to obtain a refund. This will lead to restraining sales and causing an excessive influx of waste in the regions that adopt the scheme. Another problem is the additional cost of giving a refund to customers who did not pay the initial deposit. To avoid these problems and to operate a deposit-refund scheme effectively, it is important to implement the scheme across regions as broadly as possible.

7.3.2 *Penal Regulation as a Substitute for a Deposit-Refund Scheme*

So far, we understand that a deposit-refund scheme rewards responsible disposal and recycling and discourages illegal dumping and the mixing of hazardous waste with ordinary solid waste. While applicable to a broad range of waste types, a deposit-refund scheme may be infeasible in situations where waste sources are difficult to track, as in the case with household wastes where miscellaneous items and materials are placed in a single trash bag. In this case, penal regulations, which impose penalties and fines on illegal dumpers, are suitable to reduce illegal dumping.

For the regulations to effectively reduce illegal dumping, it is crucial to set penalties and fines at optimal levels; if they are small, illegal dumping will not be reduced. Below we will consider an optimal fine for illegal dumping that would achieve the social optimum. By the term "fine," we refer to a sum of money that the polluter pays as a penalty, which includes clean-up costs and restoration costs among others.

The optimal fine imposed on the polluter is equal to the social costs of illegal dumping such as environmental damage and environmental restoration costs, if the detection probability of illegal dumping is 100%. However, in reality, it is difficult to monitor and detect every single case of illegal dumping. Fines need to be set depending on the detection probability. Because if the probability is low, the expected costs of illegal dumping to the polluter (i.e., the detection probability multiplied by fines on illegal dumping) becomes low and hence, so does the incentive to refrain from illegal dumping.

Then what conditions should be set for the optimal fines? To answer the question, we need to consider the dumper's benefits and costs, where "benefits" mean avoiding disposal and recycling fees and "costs" mean legal liabilities to pay a fine. Individuals may choose illegal dumping over proper disposal if benefits exceed expected costs. That is, incidents of illegal dumping do not decrease as long as the expected costs remain small.

From our discussion of environmental taxes in Chap. 2, we know that improper or illegal dumping gives rise to a negative externality. Therefore, the external costs caused by the disposal of waste (i.e., costs to clean up the site to restore the environment to its original condition) should be reflected in the fine. If we set the fine equal to the external costs, the expected costs of illegal dumping will be smaller than the actual external costs. Because we cannot detect all incidents of illegal dumping.

Suppose that the external costs are JPY 100 million and the detection probability is 50%. Then the expected costs are JPY 50 million, which is smaller than the external costs. To control illegal dumping at the optimal level, the fine must be set such that the dumper's expected costs are equal to the external costs. Therefore, the condition of the optimal fine is

$$\text{(Optimal fine)} = \frac{\text{(External costs)}}{\text{(Detection probability)}}$$

If the external costs are JPY 100 million and the detection probability is 50%, the optimal fine is JPY 200 million (i.e., JPY 100 million divided by 0.5). Polluter's incentive for illegal dumping will be reduced by setting the fine as follows: the higher the detection probability, the lower the fine should be, and vice versa, the lower the probability, the higher the fine should be. In either case, the fine needs to be set higher than the external costs since the detection probability is lower than 100%. It is also necessary to concurrently introduce measures aimed at improving the detection probability. It should be noted that penal regulations incur additional costs, such as monitoring and administrative costs associated with introducing surveillance cameras and patrol services.

These costs are unnecessary with a deposit-refund scheme, which is one of its advantages compared to other alternative measures, including penal regulations. Another advantage is that the collected revenues, namely, the deposit that a person paid but did not get refunded due to illegal dumping, can be used to clean up contaminated sites and restore the environment. Loss of the deposit due to illegal dumping can be regarded as a penalty on the illegal dumpers. Under a deposit-refund scheme, the financial burden is borne by individuals or businesses that commit improper action.

Given these advantages, a deposit-refund scheme should be adopted more comprehensively, applying to as many types of waste as possible. At present, the End-of-Life Vehicle Recycling Act incorporates a deposit-refund scheme and effectively discourages illegal dumping of used vehicles while promoting the reduction and recycling of ASR. On the other hand, this scheme is not adopted to collect home appliances in Home Appliance Recycling Act and as a result, illegal dumping often occurs. Given the environmental problems caused by illegal dumping and the cost of enforcement, the use of a deposit scheme should be considered in the future.

Reference

Jambeck, J., Geyer, R., Wilcox, C., Siegler, T., Perryman, M., Andrady, A., Narayan, R. and Law, K. (2015) "Plastic waste inputs from land into the ocean", Science, 347(6223), 768–771. https://doi.org/10.1126/science.1260352

Chapter 8
Air Pollution in Japan and the World

Toshi H. Arimura

Abstract This chapter explores air pollution issues in Japan and the world. It reviews pollution problems caused by air pollutants such as sulfur dioxide (SO_2) and suspended particulate matter (SPM). The chapter also discusses Japanese air pollution policy measures, including sulfur charges and vehicle type regulations, from an economic perspective. The discussion then moves to air pollution in the world. Household air pollution in developing economies and related issues are discussed in the broader context of SDGs.

Keywords Air pollution · SO_2 · SPM · $PM_{2.5}$ · PM_{10} · NOx · Household air pollution · Sulfur surcharge · Vehicle type regulation · Air pollution policy in Japan

8.1 Introduction

Since the coronavirus pandemic began in 2020, so many lives have been lost and economic activities were severely affected by the large-scale restrictions such as lockdowns and travel bans. Meanwhile, these measures brought some positive impacts on the environment. The U.S. EPA AirData shows that the air quality in Los Angeles was the cleanest in decades during the pandemic's first year (CNN, April 7, 2020[1]). Likewise, the level of air pollutants in Southeast Asia decreased by 40%, according to the World Meteorological Organization (UN News, September 3, 2021[2]). The improvement in air quality was dramatic but might be short-lived. Air pollution remains a serious problem especially in non-OECD developing economies. According to the OECD estimates (2014), the economic costs of health damage by air pollution in China and India are $1.4 trillion and $0.5 trillion, respectively, and these combined costs are greater than those of all OECD countries ($1.7 trillion).

---

[1] Kann, D (2020, April 07) Los Angeles has notoriously polluted air. But right now it has some of the cleanest of any major city. CNN. https://www.cnn.com/2020/04/07/us/los-angeles-pollution-clean-air-coronavirus-trnd. Accessed 02 January 2024.

[2] Air quality improvements from COVID lockdowns confirmed. (2021, September 03) UN News. https://news.un.org/en/story/2021/09/1099092. Accessed 02 January 2024.

T. H. Arimura and A. Hibiki, *Introduction to Environmental Economics and Policy in Japan*, https://doi.org/10.1007/978-981-97-2187-0_8

The OECD's estimates, updated in 2016, indicate that the world's economic losses from air pollution would increase to \$18–25 trillion by 2060. The welfare losses from premature deaths caused by air pollution are estimated to be about \$3.4–3.5 trillion by 2060 in the OECD countries, a sharp rise from \$1.4 trillion in 2015, and an even greater number of losses is expected in non-OECD countries. Air pollution has been serious especially in non-OECD Asia over the last ten years. Beijing is known as a city with one of the highest levels of air pollution mainly due to coal combustion that causes $PM_{2.5}$ emissions. High concentrations of $PM_{2.5}$ have been observed in Seoul as well. Mumbai and Delhi are among the top list of cities with the worst air quality. The air in Ulaanbaatar, the capital of Mongolia, is severely polluted in winter due to the burning of coal for heat at home.

Polluted air caused environmental and health risks also in Japan during its rapid economic growth in the 1960s and 1970s (see Chap. 2 for details). The pollution levels started to drop significantly after regulatory policies were implemented in the mid-1970s. Presuming that Japan's experience of overcoming the problem serves as a reference for developing countries facing air pollution, we will review some of the key policies and regulatory standards adopted by the Japanese government. In the following section, we will provide background information about air pollution by identifying its sources, causes, and health effects. We will then review air pollution problems in Japan and discuss the nation's countermeasures and the extent to which they contributed to improving the air quality. Finally, we will turn to the current situations in non-OECD countries, especially in Asia where air pollution is a serious concern both in outdoor and indoor environments.

8.2 Sources, Causes, and Health Effects of Air Pollution

Air pollution is primarily caused by the combustion of fossil fuels (e.g., coal, oil, and natural gas) that contain sulfur. When these fuels are burned, sulfur is oxidized to form sulfur dioxide (SO_2), one of the primary air pollutants that causes health problems such as bronchitis and asthma. Fossil fuel combustion also produces nitrogen oxides (NOx), another primary air pollutant, which is formed by the oxidation of nitrogen in the fuels. NOx is generated also when automobile engines and boilers in factories are heated, causing nitrogen and oxygen in the air to combine. Usually existing in the air as nitrogen monoxide and nitrogen dioxide, NOx causes harmful effects on lungs. It reacts with organic compounds emitted from factories and automobiles in the presence of ultraviolet light (UV) in sunlight and forms photochemical oxidants. They cause photochemical smog that results in health hazards such as headaches, breathing difficulties, and painful irritation of the eyes and throat.

SPM, VOCs, and $PM_{2.5}$ also cause air pollution and respiratory diseases. SPM, or suspended particulate matter, is particulate pollution suspended in the air whose size is 0.01 mm or less. It comes from a wide variety of sources, including soot from fuel burning in factories and natural sources such as yellow dust from China. Volatile organic compounds (VOCs), such as xylene, toluene, and ethyl acetate, are a general term for organic compounds that are volatile and become gaseous in the atmosphere. VOCs produce SPM and photochemical oxidants, which are, again, major causes of air pollution and health effects. Sources of VOCs emissions include automobile exhaust gases and the evaporation of fuels, solvents, and paints from factories. $PM_{2.5}$ refers to fine particles whose diameters are 2.5 μm or smaller. Soot, dust, and sulfur oxides generated in factories are the major causes of the particles.

These harmful pollutants were widespread in Japan when heavy chemical industry played the leading role in industrialization. SO_2 caused the Yokkaichi asthma outbreak, one of the major pollution diseases that occurred in the 1960s.[3] Photochemical smog was formed frequently in the 1970s, especially in the *Kanto*[4] and *Kinki*[5] regions. Although the occurrences of smog have decreased at present, the problem has not been resolved completely; photochemical smog alerts were issued as recent as in 2021. SPM and $PM_{2.5}$ blowing in from China have still been observed widely across Japan, triggering some concerns for allergies and respiratory problems.

8.3 Air Pollution and Policy Measures in Japan

Given its impact on the environment and public health, air pollution is listed first of the seven major types of pollution in the Basic Environmental Law that serves as the national guidelines for formulating environmental policies in Japan. Air pollution severely affected the lives of Japanese residents, especially those who lived in industrial areas or near streets with heavy traffic. Residents of Yokkaichi suffered from respiratory ailments such as chronic bronchitis, bronchial asthma, and pulmonary emphysema due to the burning of petroleum and crude oil at oil refineries and petrochemical factories. The polluted air throughout Japan led to numerous civil lawsuits against firms by victims seeking compensation from the polluter for damages that exceed the "tolerable limit." (ERCA 1997).

The victim's transaction costs (i.e., costs associated with bargaining with the polluter)[6] were significant back then because the civil law stipulated that the obligation to pay compensation for damage arises only when the polluter was found to have been intentional or negligent. That is, compensation would not be paid to the victim unless it was proven that his or her health damage was caused by the polluter's willful misconduct or negligence. Many victims still opted to file lawsuits. In response to an ever-increasing number of pollution victims and lawsuits, the government enacted the Pollution-Related Health Damage Compensation Law in 1973 as a relief measure for

[3] Yokkaichi asthma is one of the four major pollution diseases in Japan and the only one caused by air pollution; the other three (Itai-Itai disease, Minamata Disease, and Niigata Minamata Disease) were caused by water pollution.

[4] Kanto region includes the Tokyo metropolitan area.

[5] Kinki region includes the Osaka metropolitan area.

[6] See Chap. 3 for details on transaction cost and the Coase theorem.

the victims. Consequently, transaction costs of the victims were significantly lowered as they no longer had to prove the polluter's misconduct or negligence.

With the aim to implement countermeasures effectively and comprehensively, the government also established the Environmental Agency, which is the former body of the Ministry of the Environment (MOE) in 1971. Air quality standards were introduced subsequently in 1973 and thereafter. For example, standards for SO_2 concentrations were set that the daily average for hourly values shall not exceed 0.04 ppm, and the hourly value must be 0.1 ppm or less.

Figure 8.1 shows fluctuations in SO_2 concentrations in Japan from 1972 to 2017. SO_2 concentrations have been measured and monitored by the MOE at two types of stations: general ambient air monitoring stations (hereafter called "general stations"), indicated in the figure by the dashed line, and roadside air pollution monitoring stations (hereafter called "roadside stations"), represented in the figure by the solid line. General stations are installed in residential areas to monitor general air quality. Roadside stations are installed at intersections and nearby major roads to measure the level of pollution caused by vehicle emissions. As shown in the figure, the SO_2 levels dropped after the standards were introduced in 1973 and then significantly improved by the 1990s.

Subsequently, the standards for NO_2 were introduced in 1978, limiting the daily average for hourly values to be within or below the 0.04–0.06 ppm zone. Figure 8.2 shows fluctuations in NO_2 concentrations in Japan from 1970 to 2015. Just like SO_2, NO_2 levels are measured at general stations (represented in the figure by the dashed line) and roadside stations (represented by the solid line). Unlike what we observed for SO_2 in Fig. 8.1, NO_2 concentrations did not improve dramatically, and

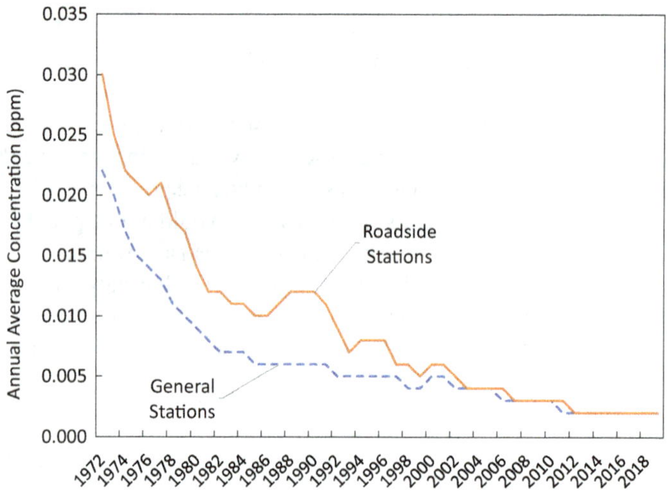

Fig. 8.1 SO_2 concentrations in Japan. *Source* MOE "FY2019 Environmental Health Surveillance for Air Pollution," adopted by the authors

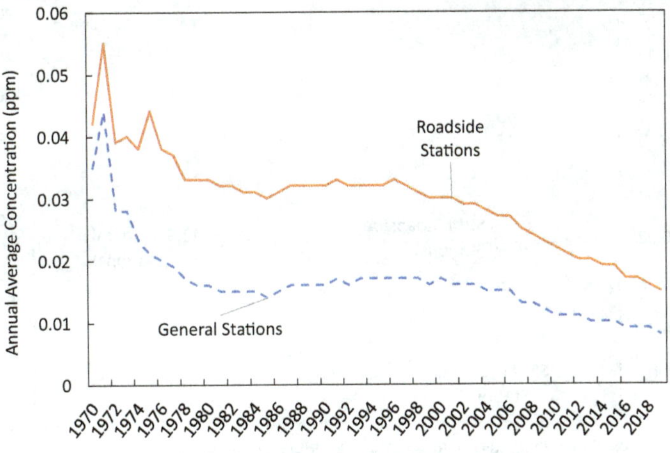

Fig. 8.2 NO_2 concentrations in Japan. *Source* MOE "FY2019 Environmental Health Surveillance for Air Pollution," adopted by the authors

they remained relatively high even in the 1990s. We will come back to discuss this point further later in this chapter.

Standards were also introduced for photochemical oxidants and SPM in 1973. Hourly values of photochemical oxidants shall not exceed 0.06 ppm. With regard to SPM, the daily average for hourly values shall not exceed 0.10 mg/m^3 and hourly values shall not exceed 0.20 mg/m^3. Much later in 2009, standards were adopted for $PM_{2.5}$: the annual standard is less than or equal to 15.0 μg/m^3, and the 24-h standard (i.e., the annual 98th percentile values at designated monitoring sites) shall be less than or equal to 35 μg/m^3.

Figure 8.3 shows fluctuations in SPM and $PM_{2.5}$ concentrations from 1974 to 2019. Similar to what we observe for NO_2, both SPM and $PM_{2.5}$ levels did not drop significantly even after the standards were introduced.

As we see in Figs. 8.1, 8.2, and 8.3, the levels of all pollutants were higher at roadside stations than general stations, indicating that air pollution is more severe in stations that are closer to emission sources. Achievement rates for photochemical oxidants are extremely low; only 0.2% of the monitoring stations (2 of 1,166 stations) managed to meet the standard. However, emissions of VOCs, which cause the generation of SPM and photochemical oxidants, have been decreasing over years. VOCs emissions are regulated under the air pollution control law, by which large sources of VOCs are designated as "VOCs emissions facilities" and emissions standards are set in accordance with facility type and size.

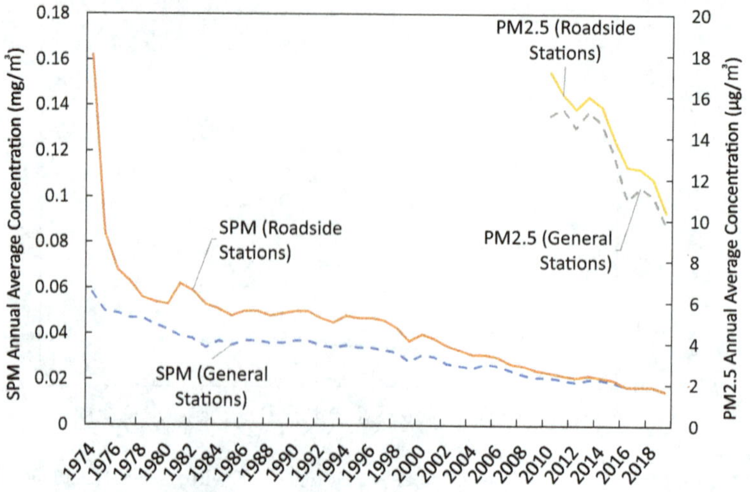

Fig. 8.3 SPM and $PM_{2.5}$ concentrations in Japan. *Source* MOE "FY 2019 Environmental Health Surveillance for Air Pollution," adopted by the authors

8.4 Air Pollution Policies in Japan

8.4.1 Point Sources

In conjunction with the air quality standards, the government and regulatory authorities imposed direct control measures. For example, based on the assumption that high concentrations of pollutants are responsible for the air pollution, the government introduced the *K-value regulation* by which industries were required to install taller smokestacks or increase the rate at which smoke from the stacks rose to dilute the concentrations. The regulation was named so because a "K-value" (where the letter K stands for the ground level concentration of SOx and its value varies from area to area (ERCA, 1997)) was included in the formula that determines the height of the stack and the velocity. The effect of making the stacks taller was limiting, given the number of factories at the time; even if individual stacks were made taller, there were too many stacks to reduce the concentrations.

Regulations were also introduced on the sulfur content of fossil fuels to control SO_2 and dust emissions. Accordingly, industries were regulated with regard to the types of fuels to use and prompted to switch to low-sulfur fuels, a more expensive alternative. They were also encouraged to adopt flue gas desulfurization (FGD), a piece of equipment that absorbs and removes SO_2 by chemical reaction before it is released from stacks. While not popular at first due to the high initial cost, FGD has made significant improvements and then became widely adopted afterwards (Fig. 8.4). It is commonly used in factories and power plants even today.

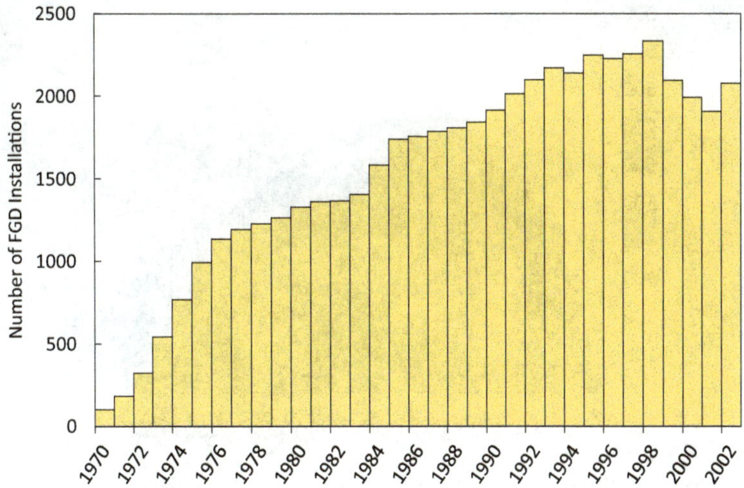

Fig. 8.4 Number of FGD installed in facilities. *Source* MOE "FY2004 Environmental Health Surveillance for Air Pollution"

Many firms have implemented FGD also because they are charged with the SO_2 levy if their emissions are greater than the specified level. Because they are monitored emissions and imposed the levy accordingly, they have the incentive to adopt FGD and lower their emissions. The levy serves as an environmental tax on SO_2 emissions, as it is charged to polluters based on their emissions volume and used to finance the compensation of the air pollution victims. The levy was introduced to 12 regions initially in 1974 and then expanded to 41 regions in 1978. The rate differs across regions. A fee per unit of pollution discharged is higher for facilities in regions where the concentrations are higher. The levy was imposed on more than 8,000 facilities and the cumulative total of compensation reached 100 billion JPY by 1978 (ERCA 1997).

Figure 8.5 shows changes in the declared amount of the levy. We can see that the amount increased in the 1970s and 1980s when the economic growth rate was relatively high. According to ERCA (1997), the imposition of the levy encouraged facilities to install FGD and thereby contributed to improving air quality in Japan. As air pollution improved, the number of victims and the amount of compensation decreased; as shown in Fig. 8.5, the total amount of compensation payments has been declining constantly since 1990.

Although the emissions decreased with more FGDs being adopted in facilities, the number of pollution patients did not decrease immediately. To compensate the same number of patients as before, the levy rate had to be increased over time. It was 15.84 JPY in Osaka when introduced first in 1974 and then surged up to 532.90 JPY by 1987. Good progress was made but nevertheless, the regulatory measures on individual firms were not sufficient to resolve the air pollution problems. The government

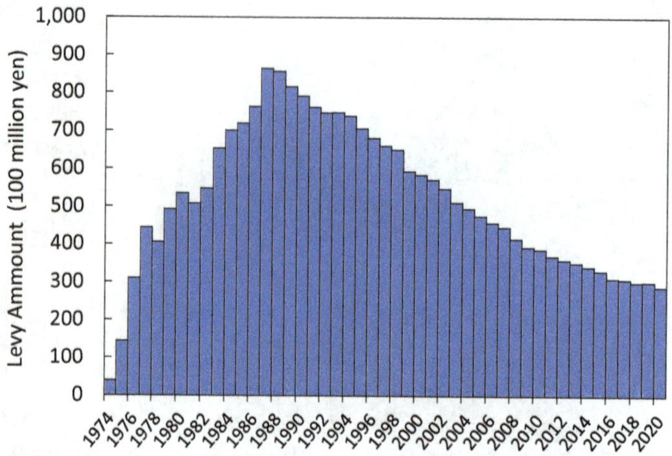

Fig. 8.5 Changes in the levy amount. *Source* ERCA (1997), "The Declared Number and Amount of the Pollution Load Levy"

thus introduced the *total emission control* and allocated emission allowances to facilities in severely polluted regions. Being vintage differentiated regulation, it imposes more stringent requirements on later entrants than on existing facilities.

8.4.2 Mobile Sources: Vehicle Emission Standards and Vehicle Type Regulations

Apart from regulations on point sources, measures were also imposed on mobile sources (e.g., gasoline and diesel vehicles), which accounted for a substantial proportion of air pollution. For example, the SO_2 levy is charged to vehicle owners as well in the form of the automobile tonnage tax, as it was stipulated that 80% of the health compensation should be financed through the levy on point sources and the remaining 20% on mobile sources when the Pollution-Related Health Damage Compensation Law was introduced. The tax is based on the weight of the vehicle, not on the distance traveled or the amount of gasoline consumed by the vehicle.

As noted earlier, while SO_2 concentrations dropped significantly (Fig. 8.1), other pollutants such as NOx and SPM did not decrease to the target levels (Figs. 8.2 and 8.3). Given that automobiles were responsible for more than half of the total NOx emissions, the government introduced a regulation known as the *vehicle unit regulation.* It applied exclusively to brand new vehicles and controlled chemical substance emissions per kilometer of vehicle travel by imposing an emission intensity limit (i.e., an upper limit on emissions generated per unit of activity).

Accordingly, standards for mobile sources were set for carbon monoxide (CO) in 1966, then for nitrogen oxide (NOx) and hydrocarbons (HC) in 1973, and finally

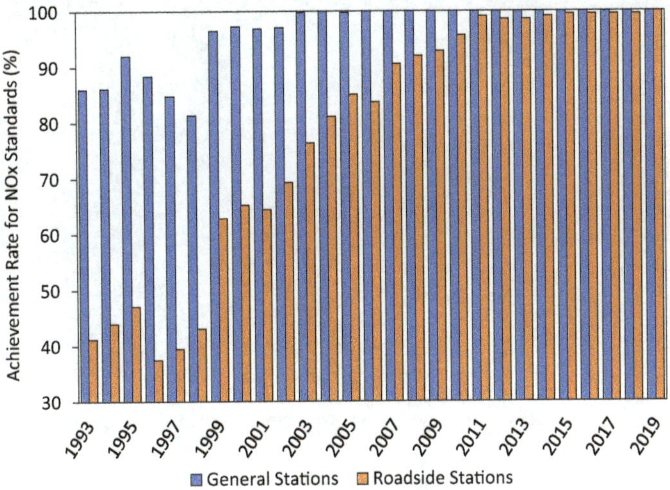

Fig. 8.6 Achievement rate for NOx standards in regions subject to the automobile NOx law. *Source* MOE "Annual Reports of Environmental Health Surveillance for Air Pollution," adopted by the authors

for suspended particulate matter (SPM) in 1993, with the target level for each pollutant becoming tighter over years. Figure 8.6 shows the achievement rate for NOx standards where the vertical axis shows the rate of achievement. We can see that the standards were not met even by the 1990s and that the rate was particularly low at roadside stations.

Figure 8.7 shows the upper limit of NOx emissions per year on a scale of 0–1.2, with 1 being the emissions volume before the standard was implemented. We can see that the emission limit has been significantly tightened over years and currently it is 0.05 as of 2021. One caveat in the regulation was that it applied exclusively to new vehicles to be sold, while there were many "old" vehicles on the road to which the standards did not apply. Because vehicles are, once sold as new, usually used for more than 10 years, the regulation did not contribute to decreasing emissions from vehicles already in use that have higher environmental impacts.

To cope with this problem, the government enforced the Automobile NOx Law[7] in 1992. Under this law, vehicles were banned from passing inspection and renewing their registration after certain years of usage. It is called *vehicle type regulation* because terminal years were determined by vehicle type. Because it is illegal to register vehicles that have failed inspection, the law directly regulated the use of old vehicles that generate higher levels of pollution. The vehicle type regulation was the nation's first and it was considered an innovative measure at the time across the world, as it was one of the first policies that restricted the use of older vehicles to curb their emissions. Implemented in 196 municipalities in 6 prefectures (Tokyo,

[7] Its official name is "the Law concerning Special Measures for Total Emission Reduction of Nitrogen Oxides from Automobiles in Specified Areas.".

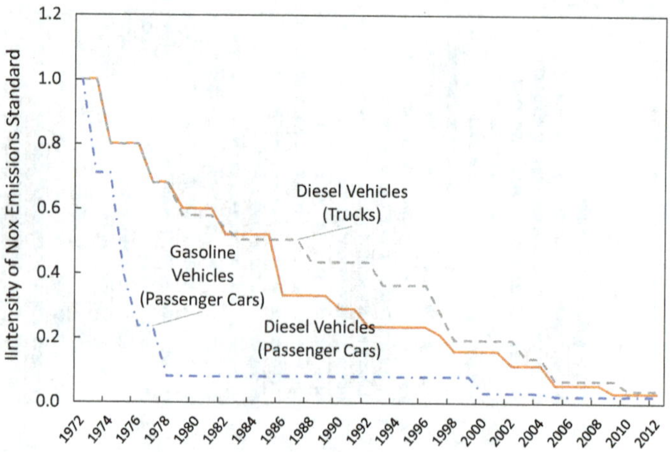

Fig. 8.7 Changes in NOx emission limits. *Source* The Osaka Prefectural Government, "FY2013 Osaka Environmental White Paper," The Ministry of Land, Infrastructure, Transport and Tourism, "Emission Regulations on New Vehicles," adopted by the authors

Saitama, Kanagawa, Chiba, Osaka, and Hyogo) where air pollution was particularly severe, the regulation aimed at promoting the replacement of old vehicles in use with new ones with better emissions standards. However, its effectiveness was limited, as shown in Fig. 8.6; the rate of achieving the target NOx (PM) level was only 43% (36%) at roadside stations in metropolitan areas in 1998.

Given that NOx concentrations did not decrease significantly and also, given the need to control PM emissions, which remained unregulated until the vehicle unit regulation was implemented in 1993, the Automobile NOx Law was revised and replaced in 2001 by the Automobile NOx/PM Law (Iwata and Arimura 2009).[8] The revision aimed at improving the concentration levels of NOx and PM. Under the new law, specified areas were extended into the Nagoya region, consisting of 276 municipalities in total. Just like its predecessor, the Automobile NOx/PM Law includes vehicle type regulation that designates the maximum age limits on vehicles.[9] The measure, together with the mandatory installation of PM removal equipment (DPF) in Tokyo and other regions, effectively improved both the concentration levels and achievement rates of NOx and PM_{10} emissions (Arimura and Iwata 2015b).

[8] Its official name is "the Law concerning Special Measures for Total Emission Reduction of Nitrogen Oxides and Particulate Matter from Automobiles in Specified Areas.".

[9] The vehicle type regulation under the Automobile NOx/PM Law was implemented in 2004.

8.4.3 Economic Analysis of Air Pollution Regulations: A Case of the Vehicle Type Regulation

Once imposed, policy measures should be assessed on their outcomes and modified as necessary to improve their effectiveness, but how can they be evaluated from an economic perspective? To demonstrate an example of economic analysis of air pollution policies, this section will present findings in Arimura and Iwata (2015a) that examine the costs and benefits of the vehicle type regulation. The regulation was implemented under the Automobile NOx/PM Law to prohibit the use and registration of vehicles, particularly freight trucks, that fail to meet specified emission standards. It sets terminal years for old vehicles in the regulated area and enforces their earlier replacement with new ones.

To comply with the regulation, vehicle owners (e.g., firms in the logistics industry) must secure financing for the earlier replacement of their old vehicles. The net present values differ depending on when they replace their vehicles, say, now as opposed to five years from now. The difference can be considered as the cost of complying with the regulation. In Arimura and Iwata (2015a), the regulation's costs are calculated by the bottom-up estimating method. That is, they first estimate the costs for individual vehicles and then aggregate the costs for all vehicles subject to the regulation to arrive at the total costs associated with implementing the regulation.

According to their estimation, the cost of a standard freight truck ranges from 150,000 to 430,000 JPY and the total costs of compliance (i.e., the costs for all regulated vehicles, including small cargo, passenger cars, and special vehicles) is 521 billion JPY. The regulation's benefits are estimated in their study by summing reductions in the external costs of both NOx and PM emissions, which was achieved by the mandatory replacement of old vehicles. According to their estimation, the benefits resulted from reducing NOx and PM_{10} emissions were 138.9 billion JPY and 1,063.4 billion JPY, respectively. The net benefits (i.e., the sum of the benefits minus the total costs) was estimated to be 681.2 billion JPY, indicating that the policy implementation resulted in a considerable net benefit to society.

It should be noted, however, that the regulation might not have been the most desirable policy option; as discussed in Chap. 2, the regulations are inefficient because the marginal abatement costs differ across polluters. The vehicle type regulation is an example of command-and-control regulations. The authors thus examine a case with an optimal policy that maximizes social surplus, namely an environmental tax, and compared its net benefit with that of the regulation. It was found that the net benefit of the tax imposition would be 1,388.4 billion JPY, almost double that of the regulation. One might argue that taxation is not a practical option because significant burden would be borne by affected parties. In response to this concern, the authors show that even a minor modification to the existing policy can make a substantial change; simply shortening the age limits of vehicles by one year would increase the net benefit by 10%. Findings in their study demonstrate that economic assessments of policy options provide policy makers with key information about them, including which option maximizes net benefit to society and whether the existing policy is implemented efficiently.

Box 8.1. Pollution Control Agreements in Japan

Pollution control agreements (PCAs) are voluntary environmental agreements (VEAs) between a local government and facilities. Japanese VEAs are one of the world's oldest experiments in voluntary policy. The first agreement was in 1952, when Shimane Prefecture signed a memorandum of understanding with the Masuda Mill of Daiwa Boseki Co., Ltd. (now Daiwabo Holdings Co., Ltd.) and the Gotsu Mill of Sanyo Pulp Co., Ltd. (now Nippon Paper Industries Co., Ltd.). In 1964, Yokohama City and Electric Power Development Co. (now known as J-Power) concluded an agreement stipulating specific and detailed numerical values. This agreement triggered the nationwide spread of PCAs.

Unlike pollution regulations based on laws and ordinances, PCAs are based on voluntary agreements; however, they are beneficial to both local governments and businesses. Local governments can take tailored and detailed pollution prevention measures that fit the needs and conditions of the regions. PCAs can also implement stricter standards (i.e., agreed values) that exceed the laws but legality will not be questioned, compared with regulations. For business operators, concluding PCAs with local governments enables them to build relationships with governments and communities and reduces resident opposition to business activities.

A detailed explanation and discussion of the Japanese PCAs can be found in Welch and Hibiki (2002) and Welch and Hibiki (2003).

(by A. Hibiki)

8.5 Air Pollution in Developing Countries

Although air pollution has improved significantly in Japan, it still poses environment and health risks globally. International Energy Agency (IEA 2023) estimates health damage from air pollution as the world strives for carbon neutrality by 2050 (see Chap. 9 for further discussion). It reports that even under the scenario of carbon neutrality, ambient air pollution caused 4.4 million premature deaths in 2022 and will cause 4.3 million premature deaths in 2025, as shown in Table 8.1. IEA also predicts that even if the world achieves carbon neutrality in 2050 and reduces the usage of fossil fuel drastically, 0.7 million people will die prematurely due to ambient air pollution. European Environmental Agency estimates that fine particulate matter

Table 8.1 Air pollution damage under net zero scenario

Premature deaths related to air pollution (million)	2022	2025	2030	2050
Ambient air pollution	4.4	4.3	2.7	2.9
Household air pollution	3.2	2.5	0.7	0.7
Share of population exposed to high levels of air pollution (>35 μg/m^3) (%)	33	29	7	7

Source IEA (2023)

($PM_{2.5}$) and NOx caused 253,000 deaths and 52,000 deaths, respectively, in EU-27 countries in 2021.[10] The problem is even more severe in emerging market and developing countries, especially in Asia. According to State of Global Air,[11] 1.85 million deaths in China and 1.67 million deaths in India in 2019 are attributable to ambient air pollution.

Among various pollutants, $PM_{2.5}$ in particular poses the greatest threat to human health (UNEP 2018). McDuffie et al. (2021) found that 1.05 million deaths worldwide could have been avoided in 2017 if fossil combustion had been eliminated, which would have resulted in the reduction of $PM_{2.5}$ emissions by 27%. As we will show in Chap. 9, coal has the highest carbon intensity per unit of energy among fossil fuels. Coal combustion for energy production and industry as well as for residential heating is the largest source of air pollution in China, accounting for 40% of $PM_{2.5}$ concentrations in 2013 (ADB 2021).

The heavy reliance on coal and biomass to meet energy needs also causes air pollution and particulate matter emissions in developing countries. For example, while India has implemented policies to shift to renewable energy, its primary energy mix is dominated by fossil fuels, with coal contributing 44%, oil 25%, and biomass 13% (ADB 2021), which increases the risk of worsening air quality in the country. According to the Paris Agreement scenario (see Chap. 9 for details), Southeast Asian countries such as Indonesia, the Philippines, and Vietnam also continue to increase coal usage to meet their energy needs (IEA 2022).

India and China have some of the most polluted cities in the world. Average annual exposure to fine particulate matter in cities such as New Delhi and Ahmedabad in India and Shijiazhuang in China is more than ten times the WHO's annual mean value: ten micrograms per cubic meter (ADB 2021). Although efforts have been made to reduce air pollution caused by vehicle emissions, inefficient diesel and two-stroke engines are still used, contributing to NOx and particulate matter emissions. In addition, the number of vehicles increased in urban areas while road capacity remains the same, resulting in more pollutant emissions per kilometer (ADB 2021).

To combat air pollution in developing countries, it might be effective to introduce a levy on pollutants, as the one imposed in Japan on SO_2 emissions. Emissions trading schemes may also be effective if they target factories and power plants. China

[10] https://www.eea.europa.eu/en/topics/in-depth/air-pollution/ (Accessed on January 1st, 2024).
[11] https://www.stateofglobalair.org/ (Accessed on January 1st, 2024).

and India introduced carbon emissions trading schemes as climate change countermeasures (see Chap. 9 for further discussion). Air quality in Beijing improved significantly after the ETS was implemented. The ETS contributed to decreasing coal consumption and consequently reduced both CO_2 emissions and air pollution. The achievement suggests that policies are more likely to be implemented and practiced effectively if they are air pollution policies complementing climate change measures, or vice versa, if they are climate change policies complementing air pollution measures.

Green vehicles (e.g., electric vehicles and fuel cell vehicles), which were not available when Japan was coping with air pollution, are a powerful substitute for conventional vehicles to curb vehicle emissions. Electric vehicles run on electricity and emit no pollutants when running. The same applies to fuel cell vehicles that uses hydrogen. If electricity is generated from renewable energy sources, CO_2 will not be produced. Promoting the use of electric vehicles can be an effective measure to reduce both air pollution and global warming. Apparently, the rapid shift to electric vehicles is due in large part to the fact that they can serve the double purpose of mitigating pollution and climate change.

8.6 Household Air Pollution in Developing Countries

Another major concern in developing countries is household air pollution. Continued exposure to household air pollutants is as harmful to public health as outdoor air pollution, as discussed in IEA's special report on energy and air pollution (2016). Household air pollution results from the use of solid fuels such as firewood and cow dung for cooking and heating. Residents of rural areas in some countries in Asia and Africa rely on solid fuels due to not having access to electricity. Incomplete combustion of those fuels in inefficient cooking stoves contributes to high PM concentrations in the indoor environment and causes respiratory health problems, ultimately leading to premature deaths. The use of candles and kerosene lamps for indoor lighting causes similar problems.

Pollution levels in kitchens in developing Asian countries often exceed the EPA guideline values. For example, the 24-h average $PM_{2.5}$ concentration in kitchens in India where solid fuels are used for cooking is reported to be about 609 mg/m^3 (Balakrishnan et al. 2013). According to WHO (2018), despite the alarming health risks of household air pollution, about 3 billion people worldwide, mainly in India and China, still rely on solid fuels to meet their household energy needs.

Commercial clean fuels are either expensive or in short supply for about 2.8 billion households worldwide (among which 500 million resides in urban regions), giving them little incentive to switching to cleaner fuels. IEA (2017) estimates that unless drastic changes are made by policy interventions, the number of people relying on polluting cooking fuels will remain largely unchanged until 2030. According to IEA (2016), almost 3 million premature deaths are linked to household air pollution annually, among which 500,000 deaths occurred in sub-Saharan Africa alone. The report predicts that 360,000 people will die prematurely by 2040, even though indoor air pollutant emissions and their damages are on a declining trend.

Improved cook stoves have been adopted as a potential solution, as they halve the consumption of firewood. However, IEA's special report points out that using improved stoves will not be a fundamental solution as it still contributes to $PM_{2.5}$ emissions. Although electrification can be another solution, technical challenges remain because power grids are not well established in developing countries, particularly in rural areas. Even if electric stoves become available, many may prefer cooking with firewood as it is considered to produce better tasting food. Practical challenges persist in the implementation of other alternatives such as solar lanterns that are difficult to cook with due to their low output.

Using firewood for cooking causes problems other than household air pollution and health damage. Deforestation due to excessive firewood harvesting is one such example. Another is gender inequalities; it is women (as well as children) who mainly engage in harvesting and collecting firewood, and the labor-intensive and time-consuming duty hinders women from entering the workforce. Household air pollution is partly attributed to poverty, health, gender, and environmental issues, all of which are included in the 17 Sustainable Development Goals. Transition to clean cooking fuels and technologies is therefore integral to achieving many points of the SDG agenda.

References

ADB (Asian Development Bank) (2021a) Greening Markets: Market-Based Approaches for Environmental Management in Asia. https://www.adb.org/publications/greening-markets-environmental-management-asia. (last access date: 10/23/2021)

Arimura, T.H. and Iwata, K. (2015a) "Ex Ante Policy Evaluation of the Vehicle Type Regulation", in An Evaluation of Japanese Environmental Regulations, Springer, Dordrecht. https://doi.org/10.1007/978-94-017-9947-8_2

Arimura, T.H. and Iwata, K. (2015b) "Cost-Benefit Analysis of Enforcing Installation of Particulate Matter Elimination Devices on Diesel Trucks", in An Evaluation of Japanese Environmental Regulations, Springer, Dordrecht. https://doi.org/10.1007/978-94-017-9947-8_3

Balakrishnan, K., Ghosh, S., Ganguli, B., Sambandam, S., Bruce, N., Barnes, D.F. and Smith, K.R. (2013) "State and national household concentrations of PM 2.5 from solid cook fuel use: results from measurements and modeling in India for estimation of the global burden of disease", Environmental Health, 12(1), 1–14. https://doi.org/10.1186/1476-069X-12-77

ERCA (Environmental Restoration and Conservation Agency) (1997) Japan's Experience of Air Pollution: Challenge to the Sustainable Development. Kogai Kenko Higai Hosho Yobo Kyokai

IEA (International Energy Agency) (2016) Energy and Air Pollution. IEA, Paris. https://www.iea.org/reports/energy-and-air-pollution. (last access date: 01/02/2024)

IEA (2017) Energy Access Outlook 2017: From Poverty to Prosperity. IEA, Paris. https://doi.org/10.1787/9789264285569-en

IEA (2022) Coal demand trends in Southeast Asia in the Stated Policies and Sustainable Development scenarios 2020–2050, IEA, Paris. https://www.iea.org/data-and-statistics/charts/coal-demand-trends-in-southeast-asia-in-the-stated-policies-and-sustainable-development-scenarios-2020-2050. (last access date: 01/02/2024)

IEA (2023) Energy access and air pollution. IEA, Paris. https://www.iea.org/reports/energy-access-and-air-pollution. (last access date: 01/02/2024)
Iwata, K. and Arimura, T.H. (2009) "Economic analysis of Japanese air pollution regulation: An optimal retirement problem under the vehicle type regulation in the NOx-particulate matter law", Transportation Research Part D: Transport and Environment, 14(3), 157–167. https://doi.org/10.1016/j.trd.2008.11.009
McDuffie, E.E., Martin, R.V., Spadaro, J.V., Burnett, R., Smith, S.J., O'Rourke, P., Hammer, M.S., van Donkelaar, A., Bindle, L., Shah, V. and Jaeglé, L. (2021) "Source sector and fuel contributions to ambient PM2.5 and attributable mortality across multiple spatial scales", Nature communications, 12(1), 3594. https://doi.org/10.1038/s41467-021-23853-y
OECD (Organisation for Economic Co-operation and Development) (2014) The Cost of Air Pollution: Health Impacts of Road Transport. OECD Publishing, Paris. https://doi.org/10.1787/9789264210448-en
OECD (2016) The Economic Consequences of Outdoor Air Pollution. OECD Publishing, Paris.https://doi.org/10.1787/9789264257474-en
UNEP (United Nations Environment Programme) (2018). Air Pollution in Asia and the Pacific: Science-based Solutions https://www.ccacoalition.org/resources/air-pollution-asia-and-pacific-science-based-solutions-summary-full-report. Accessed 02 January 2024
Welch, E. and Hibiki, A. (2002) "Japanese voluntary environmental agreements: Bargaining power and reciprocity as contributors to effectiveness," Policy Sciences, 35(4), 401–424. https://doi.org/10.1023/A:1021344508225
Welch, E. and Hibiki, A. (2003) "An institutional framework for analysis of voluntary policy: the case of voluntary environmental agreements in Kita Kyushu, Japan", Journal of Environmental Planning and Management, 46(4), 523–543. https://doi.org/10.1080/0964056032000133143
WHO (World Health Organization) (2018) Opportunities for transition to clean household energy: application of the Household Energy Assessment Rapid Tool: Ethiopia. https://www.who.int/publications/i/item/9789241514491. (last access date: 01/02/2024)

Chapter 9
International Efforts on Climate Change and Carbon Pricing in Japan

Toshi H. Arimura

Abstract This chapter provides an overview of international initiatives on climate change, including the Kyoto Protocol and the Paris Agreement, with an emphasis on the Japanese perspective. The Clean Development Mechanism (CDM) and how it led to the emergence of the Joint Crediting Mechanisms (JCM) will also be explained. Then the chapter considers the role of carbon pricing in reducing carbon emissions, explicating carbon taxes in Japan and regional emissions trading schemes in Tokyo and Saitama. After addressing design issues of carbon pricing, the chapter concludes with a discussion of Japan's carbon pricing schemes and Green Transformation (GX) policies.

Keywords Climate change · Carbon pricing · Carbon leakage · Joint crediting mechanism · The Kyoto protocol · The Paris agreement · Saitama ETS · Tokyo ETS · Green transformation (GX)

9.1 International Cooperation on Climate Change

Climate change is the greatest, most severe environmental problem confronting humankind. Of all environmental problems, climate change is the one that will affect the largest number of people and hence a challenge that must be overcome by coordinated efforts across regions and countries. The United Nations have been addressing the problem since the 1980s by setting up the Intergovernmental Panel on Climate Change (IPCC). The IPCC has released various reports on scientific findings and policy observations to lead global efforts. In its most recent report of AR 6, the IPCC urged the world to respond to the problem, concluding that "(i)t is unequivocal that human activities have heated our climate" (IPCC 2021). The section provides an overview of international initiatives on this global crisis.

T. H. Arimura and A. Hibiki, *Introduction to Environmental Economics and Policy in Japan*, https://doi.org/10.1007/978-981-97-2187-0_9

9.1.1 *International Climate Agreements: The Kyoto Protocol and the Paris Agreement*

The **Kyoto Protocol** was the world's first international agreement to reduce GHG emissions. In 1997, the Third Conference of the Parties (COP3) to the United Nations Convention on Climate Change was held in Kyoto and attended by 9,700 participants consisting of government delegates, NGOs, and press from across the world. The Protocol was adopted at this conference, setting binding targets of reducing emissions for developed countries by an average of 5.2% from 1990 levels over the 2008–2012 period. The targets have been set for each signatory nation (e.g., 6% for Japan, 7% for the U.S., and 8% for the EU) regarding the emissions of carbon dioxide, methane, dinitrogen monoxide, hydrofluorocarbons (HFCs), perfluorocarbons (PFCs), and hydrogen hexafluoride (SF6).

It can be quite challenging to have all signatories meet their targets in a growing economy and thus, the Protocol has offered flexible and cost-effective means of achieving the targets through three market-based mechanisms, namely, joint implementation, emissions trading, and **clean development mechanism (CDM)**. In particular, national emissions trading and the CDM attracted attention for their innovative designs. The CDM allows developed countries to assist developing ones financially and technologically by implementing projects in developing countries to reduce or absorb emissions. Investing countries in return are credited with emission reduction units for offsetting their emissions.

As suggested in the name of the mechanism, CDM projects must promote sustainable development in developing countries. Projects use funding from multi-financial sources, including private sectors, instead of diverting official development assistance (ODA). Emissions trading is also a reasonable market-based instrument to reduce emissions as it allows countries to cut costs associated with adopting global warming countermeasures through allowance trading (see Chap. 3 for details on emissions trading).

In the first commitment period (2008–2012) of the Protocol, Japan pledged to reduce emissions by 6% from 1990 levels. Emissions in that period increased by an average of 1.4% from the 1990 levels. The nation achieved a 3.9% reduction by using carbon sinks including forest absorption and yet it was not enough to meet the target. Hence, emissions trading was introduced for further reductions. The government obtained 94.79 million tons worth of credits, contributing to a 1.5% reduction, and private sectors obtained 274 million tons worth of credits, contributing to a 4.3% reduction, resulting in a total annual reduction of 8.4% from 1990 levels. Thanks to all the above, the target was achieved successfully.

While the Kyoto Protocol made a significant contribution by offering the international community the first opportunity to address climate change at the global level, it faced some challenges that mainly stemmed from its "**common but differentiated responsibilities (CBDR)**" principle, which means: although all countries are GHG emitters and responsible for climate change, it is developed countries that have mainly caused the problem and they should take the initiative to reduce emissions.

The principle was questioned by many parts of the world, including the U.S. who decided to withdraw from the Protocol in 2001. Even Japan, the country where the Protocol was adopted, decided not to participate in the second commitment period (2013–2020). Another problem was the Protocol's top-down approach where reduction targets were set and assigned to developed countries. The set targets met with dissatisfaction from several signatories for not being fair enough, which in turn affected subsequent international negotiations. Furthermore, it is worth noting that China and India did not have emission reduction targets under the protocol. As a result, China has become the largest emitter of greenhouse gases since the beginning of the first commitment period.

In 2015, COP21 was held in Paris where delegates from 196 regions and countries attended. There the **Paris Agreement** was adopted as a new international framework for GHG emissions reduction beyond 2020. One of the characteristics of the Agreement is that it set out a goal to limit global warming to below 2 °C compared to pre-industrial levels to avoid rapid climate change. The goal was established based on scientific input provided in the IPCC Fifth Assessment Report (IPCC 2014). IPCC released a special report (IPCC 2018) subsequently on the impacts of global warming of 1.5 °C above pre-industrial levels, which fortified the international community's effort to work toward limiting global warming to 1.5 °C.

Unlike the Kyoto Protocol that established targets for developed countries only, the Paris Agreement requires that both developed and developing countries make reduction efforts. This is because climate change action will fall short without efforts of growing economies, including China whose emissions are the largest and rapidly increasing (Fig. 9.1); if targets were imposed as in the Kyoto Protocol, it would be difficult, particularly, for developing nations to take part in the international initiatives. Hence it is obligated under the Agreement that all countries provide their climate change action plan in the **Intended Nationally Determined Contributions (INDCs)**, which are to be reviewed by other country Parties and technical experts.

Japan submitted its INDC in 2015, committing to reduce emissions by 26% from 2013 levels by 2030. Based on the input provided in the 1.5 °C special report and the Sixth Assessment Report, the nation updated the target in COP26 in Glasgow in 2021 and committed to reduce emissions by 46% from 2013 levels by 2030. When COP26 Glasgow concluded, the international community agreed to limit the rise in the global average temperature to 1.5 °C. The agreement made a big impact, having nations worldwide strive further to achieve the targets of their own by prioritizing the reduction of emissions from burning fossil fuels.

9.1.2 The Clean Development Mechanism

A key achievement of the CDM under the Kyoto Protocol was emissions reduction through the international coordination where developed countries invest in climate change mitigation projects in developing countries. For example, Japanese firms mainly in the steel and electric power industries invested heavily in China and India,

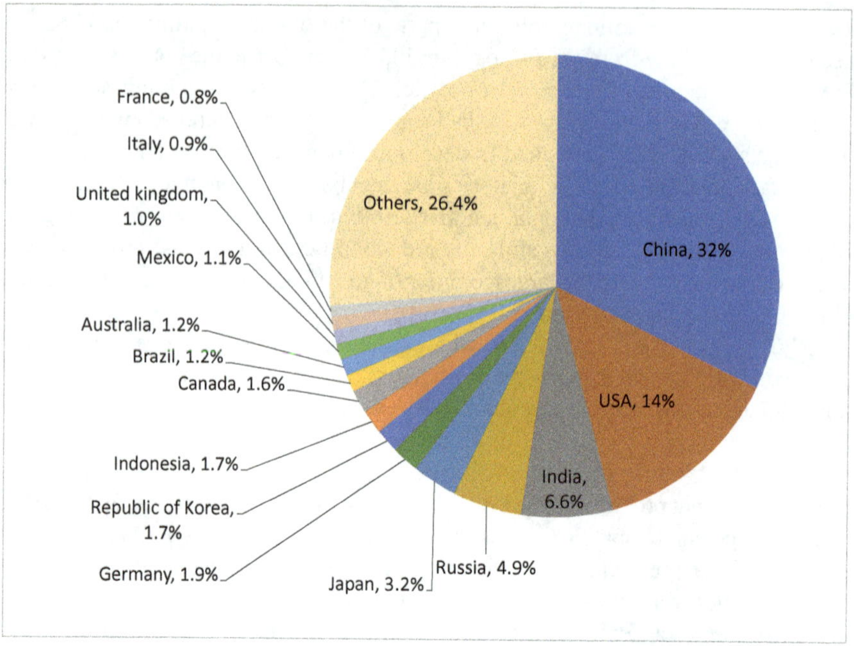

Fig. 9.1 CO_2 emissions by countries in 2020. *Source* EDMC Energy Statistics 2023

which yielded a reduction of more than 200 million tons of CO_2 in the power industry. Various CDM projects have been implemented across regions and countries. In 2011, it was estimated that 12,507 CDM projects had been registered and a total amount of emissions reduction achieved through them by 2030 would be 22.8 billion t-CO_2.[1]

At the same time, the CDM has been criticized for drawbacks, including its lengthy and laborious process for a project to be reviewed, registered, and issued with reduction credits. Once submitted, projects must undergo rigorous screening, certification, monitoring, and additional testing. All these steps contribute to long turnaround times and high workload, which might have increased transaction costs of project participants (such as firms investing in projects) and caused a decrease in the number of participating firms (Arimura et al. 2012).

Another shortcoming was the limited number of project types. Nearly half of the projects registered with the CDM Executive Board comprise wind power (25%) and hydropower (24%). In contrast, energy efficiency, which is Japan's forte, was difficult to register, as indicated by the fact that it accounts only for 5% of the registered projects. Regional distribution was another issue of concern. Figure 9.2 shows the percentage of CDM host countries that were calculated based on the number of projects as of 2021. China hosts 49% and India hosts 21% of all CDM projects, meaning that the two countries host about 70% of the total. It could be

[1] IGES CDM Project Database, https://pub.iges.or.jp/pub/iges-cdm-project-database (last access date: 12/27/2023).

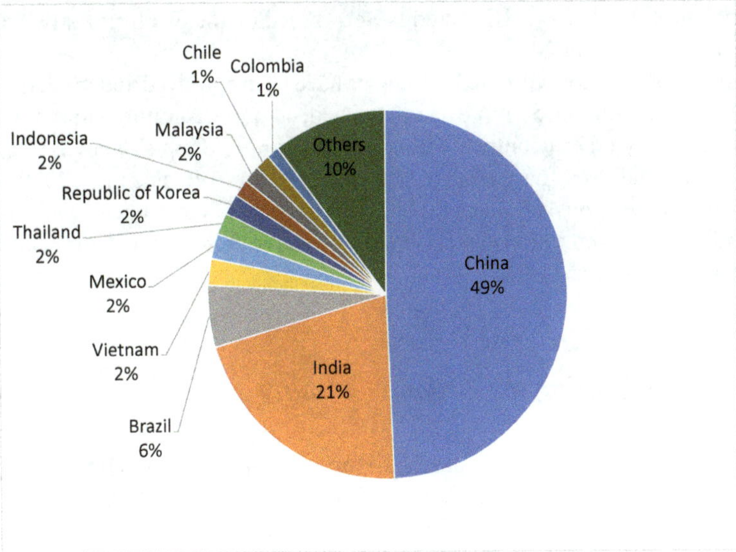

Fig. 9.2 Percentage of CDM Host countries. *Source* IGES "CDM Database"

argued that CSM projects are overly focused on China and India, despite the fact that these two countries are not the poorest. Meanwhile, CDM projects are not giving enough attention to electrification efforts in Africa.

9.1.3 The Joint Crediting Mechanism

Stakeholders in Japan, including businesses and government organizations also expressed concerns about the inadequacies of the CDM. The Japanese government dealt with the situation by implementing a program called the Joint Crediting Mechanism (JCM) (Sugino et al., 2017). The program aims to promote emissions reduction in countries that have signed bilateral agreements with Japan primarily by deploying Japan's technologies. The JCM initiative is going forward, setting out rules and procedures. For example, reduction credits issued for JCM projects are to be shared between the host developing countries and Japan. The domestic trading ruels of JCM credits have also been developed.

The JCM overcomes some of the shortcomings of the CDM. It reduces transaction costs, as projects are not necessary to go through the UN's validation and verification processes. It also allows a larger number of projects in the energy efficiency sector to be registered and conducted, thereby allowing Japanese firms to utilize their area of expertise. Starting with Mongolia, Japan has signed bilateral agreements with 30 countries as of April 2024.[2] JCM credits were issued for the first time for two projects hosted by Indonesia in 2016.

As of October 2023, JCM methodologies have been approved and implemented in 52 projects in Indonesia, 51 projects in Thailand, 44 projects in Vietnam, as well as in projects in many other countries including Mongolia, Ethiopia, Kenya, Cambodia, Bangladesh, Maldives, Laos, Palau, and Saudi Arabia.[3] Besides the 2030 goal of reducing emissions by 46% from 2013 levels, Japan aims to reduce or absorb 50 to 100 million tons of emissions by 2030 through international contributions including JCM project activities.

9.1.4 Transitioning to Carbon Neutrality

The IPCC 1.5 °C special report and the Sixth Assessment Report (IPCC 2021) have led the international community to recognize the importance of achieving net zero emissions. "Carbon neutral," i.e., having the amount of carbon released equal to the amount of carbon absorbed from the atmosphere, has become the New Gold. In December 2019, the European Commission adopted the European Green Deal to make the EU the first carbon–neutral continent in the world by 2050. When Biden assumed the U.S. presidency in 2020, the nation has set a goal to achieve carbon-free electricity by 2035 and net zero emissions economy by no later than 2050. China at the UN General Assembly in 2020 pledged to reach carbon neutrality by 2060. Russia and India also pledged to achieve net-zero carbon emissions by 2060 and 2070, respectively.

In Japan, then-Prime Minister Suga announced that the country will aim to achieve net-zero carbon emissions by 2050, which had a huge impact on Japanese industries. As of 2019, the nation's emissions from energy sources were 1,028.8 million tons of which 37.4% was from the industrial sector (such as plants and factories), 34.3% from the household and commercial sectors (such as buildings and homes), 20.0% from the transportation sector, and 8.4% from the energy conversion sector (such as electric power suppliers). While the industrial sector has the largest share, their emissions decreased by 24% from 1990 through 2019, partly as a result of their voluntary efforts on energy efficiency. While the decline in the transportation sector was only 1.2%, the improvement is noteworthy given that the household and commercial sectors increased their emissions by 35.8%.

The results point to the importance of adopting mitigation measures in the household and commercial sectors, which directly affect people's daily lives. As Japan aims to reduce emissions by 46% from its 2013 levels by 2030 along with its pledge for carbon neutrality by 2050, the nation is setting out strategic plans, with carbon

---

[2] https://gec.jp/jcm/projects/ (last access date: 30/04/2024).

[3] List of projects under the JCM Financing program by MOEJ (FY2013-2023) https://gec.jp/jcm/about/ (last access date: 01/ 27/2024).

pricing as a key instrument for fulfilling the target. The Japanese government advocated the importance of carbon pricing as drivers of economic growth, considering the initiative as opportunities to create new demand and markets. Along this line, the government promotes "**Green Transformation (GX)**," a transition to a carbon neutral economy by way of utilizing the innovation required to achieve zero emissions (For further discussion on GX, see Sect. 9.6).

9.2 The Mechanism of Carbon Pricing

Carbon pricing is gaining increasing attention as a means of achieving carbon neutrality. This section provides a brief review of the mechanism of carbon pricing—how carbon gets priced, how the market instrument promotes emissions reduction, and what impact the instrument may have on our economy both in the short and mid- to long-terms.

GHG emissions are produced by various sources (e.g., industries, transportation, and our daily activities) and as such, regulatory measures are presumably not efficient in reducing emissions. On the other hand, market-based instruments can encourage emissions reduction efficiently with minimal cost (see Chap. 3 for further details). Carbon pricing is one such instrument whereby prices are placed on carbon dioxide to curb emissions and mitigate global warming.

Although the mechanism of carbon pricing builds on the Pigouvian tax principle, the instrument does not necessarily serve as a Pigouvian tax. In the Pigouvian framework, the optimal level of carbon emissions is determined, based on which a tax is imposed equivalent to the marginal external costs. The **Social Cost of Carbon** (i.e., the cost of the damages caused by one additional ton of CO_2 emissions) has been used to quantify the marginal external costs of carbon.[4] However, it is difficult, if not impossible, to obtain accurate estimates and hence, some part of the external costs may already be internalized.

While carbon pricing puts prices on carbon that is produced as a byproduct of fossil fuel combustion, the pricing is often based on carbon content of the fuels. Pricing carbon thus causes an increase in fossil fuel prices. The extent of price increase varies by fuel type because carbon content varies by fuel type. Amounts of CO_2 per unit of energy released by coal, kerosene (oil), and gas are shown in Fig. 9.3. We can see that gas releases the lowest level of emissions followed by oil and then coal.

[4] Numerous studies have estimated the social cost of carbon using different models. For example, Nordhaus (2017) estimated the social cost of carbon (SCC) to be $31 in 2010 US$. Including human mortality impacts, Bressler (2021) updated and predicted that the SCC would range from $37 to $258 in 2020 value.

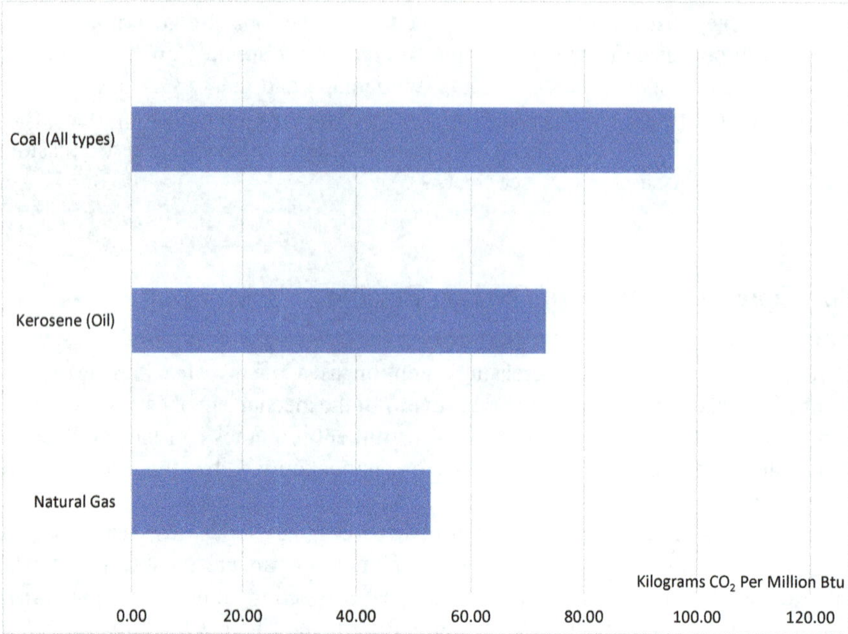

Fig. 9.3 CO_2 emissions per unit of energy produced from fossil fuels (gC/per mmBtu). *Source* US EIA (2023)[5]

9.2.1 Short- and Longer-Term Effects of Carbon Pricing

What are the effects of fuel cost increases resulting from carbon pricing? One of the short-term effects is: increased fuel prices will result in higher energy prices, raising electricity and gas bills for individual households, which in turn lead the households to change their behavior to save on energy bills (such as turning off lights more frequently and setting the thermostat higher in summer and lower in winter). Their consumption behavior will also be affected, as exemplified in the widespread adoption of LED lights—a highly energy-efficient lighting alternative—among households in response to the recent rise in electricity bills. Likewise, it is expected that energy-efficient home appliances such as refrigerators and air conditioners will become widely adopted in households. These kinds of behavioral changes will be observed in workplaces and thus will contribute to the emission reduction efforts in the manufacturing or service sector.

Carbon prices will also affect the individual's choice of transportation. As gasoline prices rise, owners of fuel-inefficient vehicles will likely switch to more fuel-efficient options such as hybrids. More people may switch from conventional fuel vehicles to electric vehicles, as they run gasoline-free and produce zero emissions if the electricity is derived from renewable energy sources. Some may choose public

[5] https://www.eia.gov/environment/emissions/co2_vol_mass.php (last access date: 12/ 27/2023).

transportation over driving cars. Friends and neighbors commuting in the same direction may start carpooling to get to their workplaces. This energy-saving practice is often adopted in the U.S. as well as Europe when gasoline prices increase.

In addition, bicycles may replace cars and motorbikes for neighborhood transportation, and bikeshare, which grew in popularity during the coronavirus pandemic, may become even more popular. All these changes in consumer lifestyles will result in decreasing emissions because less fossil fuels are to be consumed. Carpooling to and from work, for example, can halve the amount of carbon emissions. Carbon pricing is expected to accelerate emission reduction through reduced fossil fuel consumption.

Let us turn to mid- to long-term effects of pricing carbon as a climate mitigation policy. Because the carbon content of coal (natural gas) is higher (lower), its carbon price tends to be higher (lower). The difference in their carbon prices leads consumers and businesses to change their energy sources from coal to natural gas. A case in point is the U.K. power sector that went through a major shift from coal to natural gas when a Carbon Price Floor has been implemented. Another example is the U.S. shale revolution, which decreased natural gas prices and promoted the switching from coal to natural gas.

Carbon pricing is also expected to promote generating and using energy sources other than fossil fuels. If electricity and gas bills rise, renewable energy sources such as solar photovoltaic (PV) power become more economically attractive and competitive alternatives to the conventional fuels. Currently in Japan, household solar PV power generation is promoted through feed-in tariffs. Subsidies of this kind may not be needed, however, once carbon pricing is properly in place. Besides, the Japanese energy market, which has become competitive since the liberalization of the retail sector in 2016, will become even more so because the carbon pricing scheme will make renewable energy suppliers more competitive.

After the government's pledge to achieve carbon neutrality, net zero energy housing (ZEH) and net-zero energy building (ZEB) have gained attention for their energy conservation and efficiency technologies in Japan. ZEH is a construction with high thermal insulation performance combined with solar power, which enables virtually zero energy use and zero carbon dioxide emissions from housing. Although the construction cost is higher compared to conventional housing, ZEH provides health benefit of reducing temperature differences inside the house in addition to the benefit of reducing electricity consumption. Green building options like these are expected to grow further in popularity upon the implementation of carbon pricing.

Businesses will invest more in energy efficiency to reduce their emissions without reducing production. Investment in energy efficiency did increase significantly among Japanese firms after the oil crisis in 1973. More recently, the Tokyo Cap-and-Trade Program, which we will discuss below, combined with rising electricity costs after the Great East Japan Earthquake, resulted in many investments in energy conservation.

Because carbon pricing will increase demand for low-emission equipment and vehicles, the scheme is expected to stimulate businesses to make energy efficiency transitions and R&D investments. Anticipating the demand increase, the automobile sector already started R&D investment, making significant improvement in fuel efficiency, electric vehicles, and fuel cell vehicles powered by hydrogen.

Although hydrogen is attracting greater interest as a viable fuel source that does not produce any CO_2 emissions, the process to make the fuel is costly, preventing it from becoming more widely adoptable. Once carbon pricing is introduced, however, hydrogen will become a competitive alternative to conventional fuels. Firms will then foresee its widespread use and expand R&D investment in hydrogen technologies. Some may also invest in infrastructure development, particularly, to increase the number of fueling stations. Increased investment will scale up technologies, bring down costs, and promote more widespread adoption of hydrogen-based fuels.

Increased hydrogen use may also help decarbonizing energy-intensive industries and sectors such as the steel industry and coal-fired power plants. As hydrogen becomes a competitive energy source, it may replace coal in steel production and significantly reduce GHG emissions produced by the steel industry, which currently accounts for more than 10% of Japan's total emissions. Likewise, coal-fired power plants may be able to reduce emissions if they can generate power by co-firing ammonia with coal. If these transformations take place, less fuel-intensive industries will thrive, fostering technologies and skills for a green and digital economy. All these changes, by working in tandem with technological development, will serve as an efficient countermeasure against global warming.

Box 9.1 Hydrogen and Ammonia

In recent years, hydrogen has attracted considerable attention as an alternative to fossil fuels. Hydrogen, when burned, produces water but does not emit carbon dioxide, unlike fossil fuels. However, the current mainstream method of producing hydrogen uses fossil fuels, such as methane, as raw materials, leading to CO_2 emissions in the manufacturing process. Two methods are currently under consideration for mitigating CO_2 emissions during hydrogen production. First is to continue using fossil fuels as raw materials while capturing the carbon dioxide generated during production, storing it deep underground, or reusing it to reduce emissions.

The second method involves the production of hydrogen through water electrolysis. In this process, only oxygen is generated in addition to hydrogen, with no CO_2 emissions. However, electrolysis requires electricity, which can be sourced from renewable energy sources, such as solar power, making the entire hydrogen production process carbon–neutral. Therefore, renewable energy, which is difficult to store as electricity, is effectively stored as hydrogen.

Hydrogen produced by the first method is known as "blue hydrogen", while that produced by the second is termed "green hydrogen". Hydrogen production that generates CO_2 is called "grey hydrogen."

However, there are various challenges associated with hydrogen storage and transportation. The predominant storage method is compression at high pressure in metal hydrogen tanks. However, the use of hydrogen can cause metals to become brittle, which requires the use of special metals for the tanks. Additionally, hydrogen needs to be stored at very low temperatures, often below minus hundreds degrees, making the storage facilities costly. Additionally, the energy required to compress hydrogen at high pressures leads to energy loss. Hydrogen also poses safety risks because of its explosive potential when mixed with oxygen.

Ammonia has emerged as a promising energy carrier alternative to hydrogen, providing a solution to the storage and transport challenges associated with hydrogen especially in Japanese Green Transformation Strategy. When combusted using especially in Japanese Green Transformation Strategy. When combusted using modified burners, ammonia can significantly reduce nitrogen oxide emissions, thereby facilitating its use in existing coal power plants. Ammonia is synthesized from hydrogen and is classified as "blue ammonia" when produced from carbon-captured hydrogen, and "green ammonia" when using hydrogen derived from renewable energy sources.

9.2.2 Carbon Neutrality and Emissions Trading

One may think that carbon pricing will not be needed once we realize net zero emissions. Apparently, however, emissions trading, including carbon pricing, is indispensable even in a carbon neutral world. While Japan aims to achieve carbon neutrality by 2050, all economic agents in the nation do not necessarily achieve the goal by then. One can imagine that what we call "hard-to-abate industries" such as steel, cement, and petrochemicals may struggle to achievenet-zero emissions. The government takes this possibility into account in its strategic climate action plan, assuming that industrial technology that use heat may continue to consume fossil fuels to some extent and emit carbon in 2050 and onwards.

Key measures to meet the climate goal are technological solutions, particularly, technological innovation such as **carbon capture, utilization and sequestration (CCUS)** and **direct air capture (DAC)**. Natural climate solutions including forest absorption of carbon dioxide are also effective means of promoting the transition to net zero. Along with these solutions, emissions trading will play an important role; businesses and entities can realize negative emissions and earn carbon credits through CCUS, DAC, and forest carbon offsets while emitters purchase credits to offset their emissions. Adopting the combination of these technologies and solutions will be the pathway to achieve net zero emissions not only in Japan but in regions across the globe.

9.3 Carbon Pricing Developments Across the World

Carbon pricing has been adopted in a number of cities, states, regions, and nations. Below we discuss two major carbon pricing schemes: carbon taxes and emissions trading. Carbon taxes were introduced for the first time in North Europe, starting in Finland in 1990 and then in Norway, Switzerland, Ireland, and France. Carbon pricing in various forms has been adopted in the U.S. and Canada. For example, Canada implements the instrument by states and jurisdictions, as exemplified by the British Columbia carbon tax. In recent years, carbon taxes are widely adopted in other parts of the world, including Asian countries like Singapore and Latin American countries such as Mexico and Chile where climate policies are not as ambitious as in developed countries. Japan introduced a carbon tax called the Global Warming Countermeasure Tax in 2012, imposing JPY 289 per ton of carbon dioxide emissions as part of the Petroleum and Coal Tax.

After more than a decade from the launch of the first carbon tax program, an emissions trading scheme (ETS) was introduced for the first time in 2005 in Europe. Considering the success of the U.S. sulfur dioxide cap-and-trade program as part of the Acid Rain Programs, EU launched the European Union Emissions Trading Scheme (EU ETS). After a three-year pilot period, the scheme started to operate fully in 2008, targeting emissions particularly in the power sector and manufacturing industry. The program serves as a model for carbon trading programs around the world.

In the U.S., an emissions trading program across states called the Regional Greenhouse Gas Initiative (RGGI) launched in 2009, covering the electricity generating sector in ten northeastern states. Then in 2013, California's cap-and-trade program that targets key sectors of the economy was introduced and later linked with the Quebec cap-and-trade scheme. Initiatives are also taken in regions other than Europe and North America. The Mexican ETS pilot program started in 2020 and China, the world's largest emitter, introduced pilot programs in 2013 in seven cities and regions including Beijing and Shanghai. The Chinese government implemented the national ETS; a national program for the electricity generating sector launched in 2021, which is scheduled to be extended to energy-intensive industries and other sectors. Republic of Korea also introduced an emissions trading system in 2015.

Due in part to the influence of the carbon border adjustment mechanisms (CBAM: see Sect. 9.5.1 for details) proposed by the European Commission, institutional designs for putting prices on carbon are also underway in Thailand, Indonesia, Vietnam, and other ASEAN countries. EU ETS used to cover the largest volume of emissions in the world. In terms of emissions covered by a single country, Republic of Korea became the largest at once and currently, the Chinese ETS for the power generating sector has become the largest in the world.

9.4 Carbon Pricing in Japan

9.4.1 *The Global Warming Countermeasure Tax*

The Japanese carbon tax called the **Global Warming Countermeasure Tax** was introduced in 2012 and its rate is JPY 289/tCO_2 as of 2021, which corresponds to only JPY 0.76 per kilo liter of gasoline. The tax alone is not enough to induce reductions sufficiently. Thus, the government adopts a policy mix whereby the carbon tax is imposed in combination with subsidies; the tax revenues that amount to JPY 234 billion in the FY2021 budget are used to subsidize renewable energy and energy-efficient technologies. Although the tax may be considered as a burden on firms and consumers, it means an increase in the government revenue, which, if used effectively, can benefit the economy while promoting emissions reductions. It should be noted, however, that the current tax rate is too low to achieve net zero emissions by 2050. European countries have a higher level of carbon tax. For example, in 2023, the carbon tax in France is US$48.5 and it is $125.56 per in Sweden.[6]

9.4.2 *Sub-national Emissions Trading Schemes*

While the decision to implement a national ETS was postponed in Japan in 2010, emissions trading programs at the sub-national level were launched first in Tokyo and then in Saitama (Arimura and Matsumoto, 2020). Tokyo ETS, introduced by the Tokyo Metropolitan Government, was the first cap-and-trade program of CO_2 emissions in Asia. It differs from the preceding programs (such as EU ETS and RGGI) in that it is tailored to reduce urban emissions by covering commercial and service sectors. This is because large-scale power plants are rarely located in Tokyo; the program targets the 1,300 large-scale facilities, majority of which are office and commercial buildings and hotels.

Initially, when Tokyo ETS was designed, the Tokyo metropolitan government faced criticisms in Japan that emission caps would be traded for profit making purposes, causing "money game" instead of serving as a climate mitigation measure (Roppongi et al. 2017). Given the criticism, the program's financial function was restricted, enabling emissions trading exclusively between target facilities. Besides, facilities are allowed to trade allowances only if they earn emissions reduction credits after reducing their emissions.

Reduction targets set for the first compliance period (2010–2014) were 8% for office and commercial buildings and 6% for manufacturing facilities from a base year level. The reductions went far beyond the targets at the end of the period, altogether achieving a 25% reduction. Some argued that this might not be due to the ETS but attributable to the increase in energy prices right after the Great East

---

[6] https://carbonpricingdashboard.worldbank.org/map_data (lase access date: 02/09/2024).

Japan Earthquake that affected multiple power plants and energy supply systems, which resulted in a serious energy supply shortage. To examine this possibility and clarify the factors contributed to the reductions, Arimura and Abe (2021) conducted an econometric analysis using data on office buildings and universities in Tokyo and decomposed the reductions into two components: the impacts of Tokyao ETS and of the energy price increase. They confirmed that Tokyo ETS did contribute to about 7% average annual reduction in the first four years.

The other subnational ETS program launched in 2011 in Saitama, a prefecture located north of Tokyo, targeting 600 facilities. It is linked with Tokyo ETS, but unlike Tokyo's program, it is a conventional type of emission capping in that the target facilities are primarily in the manufacturing sector. What distinguishes Saitama ETS from other conventional programs is that it is a voluntary scheme where no financial penalty is charged for noncompliance. In Phase II which spanned from 2015 to 2019, 618 targeted faculties achieved the reduction target by emissions reduction or by credit acquisition while only 12 facilities are incompliant.[7] This is quite distinctive compared to programs such as EU ETS and Tokyo ETS, where excess emissions and failure to obtain permits to cover emissions conventionally results in penalties. The scheme realized reductions of 22% without enforcement mechanisms in the period of four years. Hamamoto (2021) conducted an econometric analysis of Saitama ETS and found that the system promoted the adoption of energy efficient technologies in the targeted facilities. Both Tokyo and Saitama programs contributed to significant reductions at the end of the first compliance period in 2014, and they functioned well in the second period (2015–2019). As of 2024, they are now in the third period, making steady progress toward long-term reductions.

9.4.3 *J-Credit Scheme: A Voluntary Emissions Reduction Certification Program in Japan*

The Japanese government introduced a domestic credit certification scheme called the Japan Greenhouse Gas Emission Reduction Certification Scheme (J-Credit Scheme) in 2013 to promote voluntary initiatives to reduce emissions in Japan. In contrast to the cap-and-trade system described in Chap. 3, the J-credit system is a baseline and credit system. For this scheme, we first calculate the baseline emissions assuming no mitigation effort is made. Then, we calculate the emission level when mitigation efforts are implemented. Entities can receive the credits for the difference between the baseline emissions and the actual emissions. That is, domestic entities can receive and sell credits by reducing emissions through energy saving, renewable energy, and forest carbon sink. Entities can use the credits to achieve their targets set in accordance

[7] https://www.pref.saitama.lg.jp/a0502/sakugen.html (last access date: 12/28/2023).

with the *Keidanren*[8]'s Commitment to a Low Carbon Society. They can also reduce their emissions by reporting the credits earned in the mandatory GHG Accounting and Reporting System.

The scheme achieved 9.29 million tons of CO_2 reductions, having 1,049 projects registered as of January 2024. Nonetheless, demand for J-credits is not very high because entities do not have strong incentive to earn credits because there has been no mandatory emissions reduction scheme at the national level. The low demand for credits (and hence the small number of credits being issued) decreases market liquidity, making unclear the level of carbon prices under the scheme.

9.5 Designing Carbon Pricing Systems

Although pricing carbon is an effective climate measure that internalizes market externalities, practical challenges exist in implementing the instrument. They can be overcome, however, by utilizing tax revenues and ETS auctioning revenues, which in turn will create opportunities for the economy. Below we explain concerns and opportunities potentially arising from carbon pricing.

9.5.1 Carbon Leakage and International Competitiveness

A major concern about carbon pricing is that it may cause industries to relocate to unregulated countries and result in carbon leakage, reducing domestic emissions while increasing emissions elsewhere. Besides, energy-intensive industries (such as the steel industry) may be put in a vulnerable position and lose their international competitiveness against unregulated firms. These are the concerns expressed in Japan when a national ETS was proposed and extensively discussed at the Ministry of the Environment (MOE)'s Council and the Emissions Trading Subcommittee. Facing opposition from energy-intensive industries, the cabinet decided to postpone the scheme in 2010.

Minimizing the risk of carbon leakage and safeguarding the international competitiveness of domestical industries are key to adopt the scheme successfully. As such, research has been conducted to identify the most severely affected sectors as well as emission allowance allocation to prevent carbon leakage (Dechezleprêtre and Sato 2017). So far, evidence of carbon leakage is weak or absent (Colmer et al. 2023). Meanwhile, the EU ETS has been dealing with the risk of carbon leakage by allocating allowances free of charge to *energy-intensive trade-exposed* (EITE) sectors.

---

[8] *Keidanren* is also known as *Japan Business Federation*. It is the most comprehensive industrial organization that consists of 107 nationwide industrial associations (as of 2023) such as *the Federation of Electric Power Companies in Japan* or *the Japan Iron and Steel Federation*.

An alternative solution to free allowance allocation is border adjustment policy known as the *carbon border adjustments* (CBA) by which carbon pricing is imposed on imports at the border to equalize the conditions of competition. EU first discussed CBA against the U.S. when the Bush administration withdrew from the Kyoto Protocol. The U.S. Congress also considered implementing the CBA under the Obama administration to support domestic businesses from international competitiveness, particularly against competitors in emerging countries as part of global warming countermeasures.

The CBA took a tangible form in July 2021 when the EU made a **Carbon Border Adjustments Mechanism** (CBAM) proposal as part of the **Fit for 55** package. It was proposed that the CBAM initially apply to products made in five carbon-intensive industries: steel, cement, fertilizer, aluminum, and electricity generation (and subsequently, chemicals were included). The scheme is unique in that it utilizes emissions trading, not a carbon tax, and requires importing firms purchase allowances for the emissions generated from their products.

To what extent a CBA in Japan would be effective in preventing carbon leakage while protecting domestic industries? Takeda et al. (2012) compared border adjustment policies with regard to their impacts on carbon leakage, the economy and welfare, and the international competitiveness of domestic industries. Specifically, they compared the effects of two options: border carbon adjustments and output-based rebating. Output-based rebating, also known as Output Based Allocation (OBA), offers rebates to EITE sectors rather than adjusting prices at the border (Fischer and Fox 2007). Takeda et al. (2012) indicated that the OBA is effective in reducing carbon leakage to a certain extent, though its excessive use may result in reducing overall economic efficiency.

We should point out that CBAM or CBA in general is a controversial policy instrument. CBAM may not be compatible with trade rules of the World Trade Organization. This is especially so if a government introduces exemptions on exports. CBA may be considered as subsidies. These issues are discussed form legal perspectives (Mehling et al. 2019). Furthermore, middle-income economies such as BRICS have criticized these policies as disguised protectionism.

9.5.2 The Fairness and Regressivity of Carbon Pricing

Carbon pricing is often criticized for its regressivity as it can negatively affect low-income households. The Yellow Vests Protests in 2019 in France, which was a protest against the Macron administration's deregulation measures, was driven by resentment among low-income households against the increased carbon tax, which has led to rising fuel prices. It should be noted, however, that carbon pricing is not the only policy instrument that faces the regressivity issue. The same holds for consumption taxes. One solution to the regressivity is to implement policies aimed at low-income households. Another one is a **carbon dividend,** or a policy that imposes a carbon tax to redistribute to low-income households (or, equally to all households). Carbon dividends are advocated recently; a group of conservative Republicans in the U.S. made a carbon dividend proposal in 2017 and in the U.S. congress, there was a proposal of bill by a Democratic representative in 2021.[9] Moreover, British Columbia utilizes a dividend policy to address the regressivity of carbon pricing by rebating a portion of carbon tax revenues to households.

9.5.3 The Double Dividend of Carbon Pricing

Essentially, pricing carbon can result in imposing burdens on the economy. For one thing, it increases the costs of inputs and reduces production to mitigate GHG emissions. For another, it raises production and consumption costs as it promotes the use of green energy and technologies. Nevertheless, the measure can boost economic growth by using revenues (such as carbon tax revenues and emission auction revenues) to reduce existing taxes. This revenue recycling is the **double dividend** of carbon pricing (Kolstad 2010). That is, in addition to achieving emissions reduction (which can be considered as the first dividend), the scheme provides the second dividend as it decreases the burden of conventional taxes through revenue recycling.

Conventional taxes can cause market distortions and suppress economic activity. For example, income taxes may weaken individuals' incentive to work, corporate taxes may discourage firms from investing, and the burden of social insurance cost may also discourage them from hiring new workers. Economic activity will be stimulated, on the other hand, if carbon pricing revenues are used to lower these taxes. Reduced taxes and social insurance payments are expected to result in more investment, more people working, and more firms hiring workers.

The double dividend principle has been adopted in many parts of the world, including Northern Europe and North America. Germany also adopted it when introducing an energy tax reform in 1999. As mentioned above, so did British Columbia when implementing carbon pricing; since the scheme launched in 2008, the revenue has been used to cut the corporate tax, among others, generating a 0.74% annual increase in employment over the 2007–2013 period (Yamazaki 2017). If a carbon tax is to be introduced in Japan, it is desirable to recycle the revenue and obtain double dividends. By partially distributing its revenue to lower, say, the corporate tax, a carbon tax is expected to promote the green economy and economic growth while achieving emissions reductions (see Takeda and Arimura (2021) for further discussion on prospects for carbon taxes and double dividends in Japan).

---

[9] "H.R.2307—Energy Innovation and Carbon Dividend Act of 2021" https://www.congress.gov/bill/117th-congress/house-bill/2307 (last access date: 01/17/2024).

9.5.4 Effective Carbon Rates and Challenges of the Current Energy Taxes

With the aim of providing a comprehensive analysis of carbon pricing within and across countries, the OECD introduced the **effective carbon rates** (ECR), which measure the price of carbon emissions resulting from fossil fuel taxes, feed-in tariffs, as well as carbon taxes and ETS (OECD 2023). They are included as part of the carbon price because reduction incentives are provided not only through the explicit carbon pricing like a carbon tax and ETS but also through energy taxes.

In the case of Japan, incentives have been provided through fossil fuel taxes that were imposed prior to the carbon tax. Nevertheless, according to the MOE's estimates based on the OECD (2019), Japan's national average ECR remains relatively low among developed countries. This is partly caused by the nation's current carbon pricing schemes. While fossil fuel taxes have been in place, the rates per carbon content considerably differ across fuel types, making emissions reduction inefficient (Fig. 9.4). As of 2021, the rate for gasoline is JPY 24,241 while for LPG is JPY 6,524, which is still high compared to those of heavy fuel oil (JPY 1,667), natural gas (JPY 1,556), and coal (JPY 998). It is desirable to standardize the rates for more effective reductions. It is also noteworthy that coal is taxed at a rate much lower than the other fuels. The lower tax rate not only results in inefficient reduction but also allows for loopholes that can increase coal demand, in turn increasing carbon emissions. It may have also caused the concerns that the electricity deregulation can lead to an increase in coal power generation in Japan.

9.6 Carbon Pricing for Carbon Neutrality: Japan's Green Transformation (GX)

Although Japan lagged behind Korea and China, let alone the EU, in introducing an effective national-level carbon pricing scheme, the nation is moving forward on developing the initiative since the carbon–neutral pledge has been made by Prime Minister Suga in 2020.[10] The government has modified its view on climate policies, perceiving that properly designed policies will foster technological innovation and the nation's economic growth. Based on this recognition, the government introduced the concept, "Green Transformation (GX)," and maintained that the implementation of measures against climate change provides opportunities for accelerating innovations to realize a carbon–neutral economy. In other words, the government focuses on the positive side of climate policies and considers carbon pricing not as a cost for the economy but as a driving force of economic growth.

---

[10] Please refer to Arimura and Matsumoto (2021) for the discussion on carbon pricing in Japan before the carbon neutral pledge.

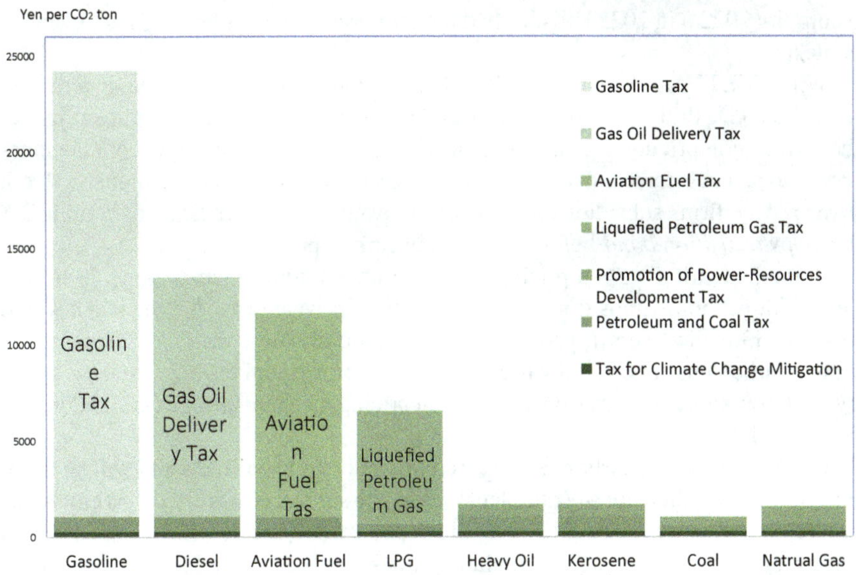

Fig. 9.4 Tax rates per carbon content in Japan. *Source* MOE (2020), adapted by the authors. *Note* The detailed tax rates are as follows. Tax for climate change mitigation is 289 yen for all fuel types. Petroleum and coal tax differs by fuel type: 400 yen per CO_2 ton for LNG/Natural Gas, 301 yen for Coal and 779 yen for others. Promotion of power-resources development tax varies by fuel type: 599 yen for heavy oil and kerosene, 408 yen for coal and 877 yen for natural gas

The GX initiative involves Japanese firms that support carbon pricing and climate policy due partly to the Task Force on Climate-related Financial Disclosures (See Box 9.2 for more details on TFCD). It also led to the emergence of the GX league, a platform where firms with ambitious GHG emission targets are invited to discuss ways to develop, practice, and implement green transformation. Firms in the league can participate in the GX-ETS where they can voluntarily conduct emissions trading. Moreover, they were able to participate in rulemaking for the GX-ETS and thereby contribute to the collaborative effort of creating new markets. Anticipating a mandatory emissions trading scheme, 568 firms participated in the GX-ETS, representing more than 50% of Japanese emissions. Firms participating in the league include the nation's major power companies and steel companies. The first phase of the GX-ETS launched in 2023 and continues until 2025. The Ministry of Economy, Trade and Industry (METI) supported this initiative by commissioning to the Tokyo Stock Exchange to set up a carbon market, and the market launched in 2023. METI also established a study group to prepare carbon credits for carbon neutrality. The group published "Carbon Credit Report[11]" (Study Group on Preparation of Operational Environment to Ensure Proper Use of Carbon Credits toward Achieving Carbon

[11] https://www.meti.go.jp/shingikai/energy_environment/carbon_credit/pdf/20220627_2.pdf (last date access 02/09/2024).

Neutrality 2022)) in 2022 and clarified the proposed use of carbon credits in various contexts.

While METI was establishing the GX league and the GX-ETS, the government passed the GX Promotion Act in May 2023. Under this act, the government implements a carbon pricing scheme while providing funding to firms to encourage innovation to achieve carbon neutrality. The government's approach is unique in that it gives private firms subsidies for R&D or innovation to private firms by issuing *GX economy transition bond* before introducing carbon pricing.

In implementing carbon pricing, the government committed to issue 20 trillion yen of GX economy transition bonds in support of private firms, hoping that it would lead to 150 trillion yen in private investment, an amount considered necessary to realize carbon neutral economy in Japan. The government plans to redeem the bonds by 2050 by using revenues from two carbon pricing mechanisms: GX-Surcharge and the GX-ETS.

GX-Surcharge is a carbon fee imposed on imported fossil fuels and will be introduced in 2028. While not a tax in a legal sense, the surcharge has effects on emissions reduction and economy equivalent to those of a carbon tax. It will be imposed on a wide range of economic agents, including households and small and medium sized firms. In contrast to GX-Surcharge, the GX-ETS targets larger emitters such as the power sectors and other energy-intensive sectors. It is stipulated that an auction of permits will be introduced under the GX-ETS for the power sector in 2033. It is natural that the power sector will pay for permits through auction as in the case of EU ETS and that the GX-ETS, initially starting on a voluntary basis, will eventually evolve into a mandatory system.

As of January 2024, the details of carbon pricing under the GX law are yet to be determined. While the national government has formulated the grand design of carbon pricing for carbon neutrality, the devil is in the details. We are yet to find out when the voluntary participation to the GX-ETS will become mandatory and what level of GX-Surcharge will be imposed. In designing carbon pricing policies, the government needs to consider how best to address various issues that we discussed in the previous section. It is important to keep an eye on the further development of carbon pricing in Japan.

Box 9.2 The Role of Non-state Actors in Climate Change Mitigation

The Trump administration in the United States marked a significant crisis in international cooperation on climate change. Adhering to a typical Republican stance, the administration quickly declared its intention to withdraw from the Paris Agreement. Additionally, it favored resolving issues through bilateral negotiations and raising tariffs over multilateral coordination through international organizations. This increase in anti-globalism has diminished the capacity of nations to resolve international issues.

During this period, **non-state actors** became increasingly significant as alternatives to national governments. Non-state actors are organizations other than nation-states, including corporations, NGOs, and local governments, that historically are not directly involved in international negotiations. With the increasing complexities in international affairs, the role of non-state actors in addressing various issues, including climate change, has garnered attention.

For instance, in the United States, several state governments have introduced emissions trading schemes. In the northeastern states, including New York, a system called RGGI-targeting power plants was introduced, and California implemented an emissions trading scheme. In Japan, Tokyo introduced emissions trading, followed by Saitama Prefecture. Thus, state governments, local authorities, and regional leaders have begun to play significant roles.

One symbolic figure of non-state-actor involvement is Michael Bloomberg. Known both as the former mayor of New York City and the founder of a financial information service, Bloomberg has been actively engaged in climate change mitigation. In 2014, he co-founded the "Global Covenant of Mayors for Climate and Energy" with then-UN Secretary-General Ban Ki-moon and served as the UN Secretary-General's Special Envoy for Climate Ambition and Solutions.

Non-State actors also play a critical role in financing. Mark Carney, former Governor of the Bank of England, collaborated with Bloomberg to promote the disclosure of climate change-related risks faced by financial institutions. This initiative led to the formation of **TCFD** (Task Force on Climate-related Financial Disclosures), which brought significant changes to Japanese businesses and economy. With the backing of Japan's Ministry of the Environment and Ministry of Economy, Trade, and Industry, many corporations have begun disclosing their climate change risks. In Japan, when the Tokyo Stock Exchange was reorganized, compliance with the TCFD became a requirement for listing on the new Prime Market. Alongside the scientific findings of the IPCC, TCFD has played a pivotal role in advancing climate change measures taken by businesses.

The role of global corporations extends beyond financing. Companies, such as Apple, Sony, and Google, demand their suppliers to use 100% renewable energy (RE100). Progressive companies also promote decarbonization across borders.

NGOs' contributions are also noteworthy. NGOs such as WWF Japan play a significant role in advancing environmental policies in Japan. Their active participation is remarkable in advisory councils, such as the Tokyo Metropolis Environmental Council and the National Ministry of the Environment's policy councils.

Thus, amid the challenges posed by anti-globalism in international cooperation, the role of non-state actors has expanded. Today, corporate activities are becoming increasingly global, with production and markets extending beyond the confines of any country. NGOs and individuals can easily extend their activities beyond their borders by using social media. The influence of non-State actors is expected to increase in the future.

References

Arimura, T.H. and Abe, T. (2021) "The impact of the Tokyo emissions trading scheme on office buildings: what factor contributed to the emission reduction?" Environmental Economics and Policy Studies, 23(5), 17–53. https://doi.org/10.1007/s10018-020-00271-w

Arimura, T.H. and Matsumoto, S. ed. (2020) Carbon Pricing in Japan, Springer Singapore, 265 pages https://doi.org/10.1007/978-981-15-6964-7

Arimura, T.H., Miyamoto T., Katayama, H. and Iguchi, H. (2012) "Japanese firms' practices for climate change: emission trading schemes and other initiatives", Sophia Economic Review, 57(1–2), 31–54

Bressler, R.D. (2021) "The mortality cost of carbon," Nature Communications, 12, 4467. https://doi.org/10.1038/s41467-021-24487-w

Colmer, J., Martin, R., Muûls, M. and Wagner, U. J. (2023) "Does Pricing Carbon Mitigate Climate Change? Firm-Level Evidence from the European Union Emissions Trading Scheme," CRC TR 224 Discussion Paper Series crctr224_2023_232v2, University of Bonn and University of Mannheim, Germany.

Dechezleprêtre, A. and Sato, M. (2017) "The impacts of environmental regulations on competitiveness", Review of environmental economics and policy, 11(2), 183–206. https://doi.org/10.1093/reep/rex013

Fischer, C. and Fox, A. K. (2007) "Output-Based Allocation of Emission Permits for Mitigating Tax and Trade Interactions", Land Economics, 83(4), 575–599. https://doi.org/10.3368/le.83.4.575

Hamamoto, M. (2021) "Impact of the Saitama Prefecture target-setting emissions trading program on the adoption of low-carbon technology", Environmental Economics and Policy Studies, 23, 501–515. https://doi.org/10.1007/s10018-020-00270-x

IPCC (Intergovernmental Panel on Climate Change) (2014) Climate Change 2014: Synthesis Report. Contribution of Working Groups I, II and III to the Fifth Assessment Report of the Intergovernmental Panel on Climate Change [Core Writing Team, R.K. Pachauri and L.A. Meyer (eds.)]. IPCC, Geneva, Switzerland. https://epic.awi.de/id/eprint/37530/1/IPCC_AR5_SYR_Final.pdf. (last access date: 01/12/2024)

IPCC (2018) Global Warming of 1.5°C. An IPCC Special Report on the impacts of global warming of 1.5°C above pre-industrial levels and related global greenhouse gas emission pathways, in the context of strengthening the global response to the threat of climate change, sustainable development, and efforts to eradicate poverty [Masson-Delmotte V, P Zhai, H-O Pörtner, D Roberts, J Skea, PR Shukla, A Pirani, W Moufouma-Okia, C Péan, R Pidcock, S Connors, JBR Matthews, Y Chen, X Zhou, MI Gomis, E Lonnoy, T Maycock, M Tignor, and T Waterfield (eds.)]. Cambridge University Press, Cambridge, UK and New York, NY, USA. https://doi.org/10.1017/9781009157940.001

IPCC (2021) Climate Change 2021: The Physical Science Basis. Contribution of Working Group I to the Sixth Assessment Report of the Intergovernmental Panel on Climate Change [Masson-Delmotte V, P Zhai, A Pirani, SL Connors, C Péan, S Berger, N Caud, Y Chen, L Goldfarb, MI Gomis, M Huang, K Leitzell, E Lonnoy, JBR Matthews, TK Maycock, T Waterfield, O Yelekçi, R Yu, and B Zhou (eds)]. Cambridge University Press, Cambridge, UK and New York, NY, USA. https://doi.org/10.1017/9781009157896

Kolstad, CD. Environmental Economics 2nd Edition Oxford University Press

Mehling, M., Van Asselt, H., Das, K., Droege, S., and Verkuijl, C. (2019) "Designing Border Carbon Adjustments for Enhanced Climate Action", American Journal of International Law, 113(3), 433–481. https://doi.org/10.1017/ajil.2019.22

Nordhaus, W.D. (2017) "Revisiting the social cost of carbon," Proceedings of the National Academy of Sciences, 114 (7), 1518–1523 https://doi.org/10.1073/pnas.1609244114

OECD (2019) Taxing Energy Use 2019: Using Taxes for Climate Action, OECD Publishing, Paris, https://doi.org/10.1787/058ca239-en.

OECD (Organisation for Economic Co-operation and Development) (2023) Effective Carbon Rates 2023: Pricing Greenhouse Gas Emissions through Taxes and Emissions Trading. OECD Series on Carbon Pricing and Energy Taxation, OECD Publishing, Pairs. https://doi.org/10.1787/b84d5b36-en

Roppongi, H., Suwa, A. and Puppim De Oliveira J.A. (2017) "Innovating in sub-national climate policy: the mandatory emissions reduction scheme in Tokyo", Climate Policy, 17(4), 516–532. https://doi.org/10.1080/14693062.2015.1124749

Study Group on Preparation of Operational Environment to Ensure Proper Use of Carbon Credits toward Achieving Carbon Neutrality (2022) "Carbon Credit Report"

Sugino, M., Morita, M., Iwata, K. and Arimura, T.H. (2017) "Multiplier impacts and emission reduction effects of Joint Crediting Mechanism: analysis with a Japanese and international disaggregated input–output table", Environmental Economics and Policy Studies, 19, 635–657. https://doi.org/10.1007/s10018-016-0177-y

Takeda, S. and Arimura, T.H. (2021) "A computable general equilibrium analysis of environmental tax reform in Japan with a forward-looking dynamic model," Sustainability Science, 16(2), 503–521. https://doi.org/10.1007/s11625-021-00903-4

Takeda, S., Hore, T. and Arimura T.H. (2012) "Computable General Equilibrium Analysis of Border Adjustments under the Cap-And-Trade System: in Japan" in Airmura, T.H., Yomogida, M. and Kawase, T. (eds) Climate Change Policies and International Trade: Economic and Legal Analysis of Emissions Trading and Border Tax Adjustment, Tokyo, Japan, University of Tokyo Press, 87–108 (in Japanese)

US EIA (U.S. Energy Information Administration) (2023) Carbon Dioxide Emissions Coefficients. https://www.eia.gov/environment/emissions/co2_vol_mass.php

Yamazaki, A. (2017) "Jobs and climate policy: Evidence from British Columbia's revenue-neutral carbon tax," Journal of Environmental Economics and Management, 83, 197-216 https://doi.org/10.1016/j.jeem.2017.03.003.

Printed in the USA
CPSIA information can be obtained
at www.ICGtesting.com
CBHW071947210724
11924CB00003B/26

9 789819 721863